# FINDING YOUR
# LEADERSHIP
## *Style*

### A GUIDE FOR EDUCATORS

## JEFFREY GLANZ

ASCD

ASSOCIATION FOR SUPERVISION AND CURRICULUM DEVELOPMENT
ALEXANDRIA, VIRGINIA USA

Association for Supervision and Curriculum Development
1703 N. Beauregard St. • Alexandria, VA 22311-1714 USA
Telephone: 800-933-2723 or 703-578-9600 • Fax: 703-575-5400
Web site: http://www.ascd.org • E-mail: member@ascd.org

**2002–2003 ASCD Executive Council:** Peyton Williams Jr. (*President*), Raymond J. McNulty, (*President-Elect*), Kay A. Musgrove, (*Immediate Past President*), Pat Ashcraft, Martha Bruckner, Mary Ellen Freeley, Richard L. Hanzelka, Douglas E. Harris, Mildred Huey, Susan Kerns, Robert Nicely Jr., James Tayler, Andrew Tolbert, Sandra K. Wegner, Jill Dorler Wilson; Gene R. Carter, *Executive Director*.

Copyright © 2002 by the Association for Supervision and Curriculum Development (ASCD). All rights reserved. No part of this publication may be reproduced or transmitted in any form or by any means, electronic or mechanical, including photocopy, recording, or any information storage and retrieval system, without permission from ASCD. Readers who wish to duplicate material copyrighted by ASCD may do so for a small fee by contacting the Copyright Clearance Center (CCC), 222 Rosewood Dr., Danvers, MA 01923, USA (telephone: 978-750-8400; fax: 978-750-4470). ASCD has authorized the CCC to collect such fees on its behalf. Requests to reprint rather than photocopy should be directed to ASCD's permissions office at 703-578-9600.

The exercise and answers on pp. 96–98 are adapted and reprinted by permission of Joan V. Gallos from *An Instructor's Guide to Effective Teaching: Using Bolman and Deal's Reframing Organizations*. San Francisco: Jossey-Bass. (1991/1997; copyright © Joan V. Gallos). The exercise is excerpted and adapted from *Uncritical Inference Test*, copyright © 1982 by William V. Haney. Used by permission of William V. Haney. The test is available for classroom use from the International Society for General Semantics, Box 728, Concord, CA 94522 USA.

Cover art copyright © 2002 by the Association for Supervision and Curriculum Development (ASCD).

ASCD publications present a variety of viewpoints. The views expressed or implied in this book should not be interpreted as official positions of the Association.

All Web links in this book are correct as of the publication date below but may have become inactive or otherwise modified since that time. If you notice a deactivated or changed link, please e-mail books@ascd.org with the words "Link Update" in the subject line. In your message, please specify the Web link, the book title, and the page number on which the link appears.

Printed in the United States of America.

ISBN: 0-87120-692-7     ASCD Product No. 102115

ASCD member price: $21.95     nonmember price: $25.95

December 2002 member book (p). ASCD Premium, Comprehensive, and Regular members periodically receive ASCD books as part of their membership benefits. No. FY03-03.

**Library of Congress Cataloging-in-Publication Data**
Glanz, Jeffrey.
  Finding your leadership style : a guide for educators / Jeffrey Glanz.
      p.   cm.
Includes bibliographical references and index.
"ASCD product no. 102115"—T.p. verso.
  ISBN 0-87120-692-7 (alk. paper)
  1. Educational leadership—Handbooks, manuals, etc.  2.
Educators—United States—Handbooks, manuals, etc.  3. School
supervision—United States—Handbooks, manuals, etc.  I. Title.
  LB2806.4  .G5317 2002
  371.2—dc21
                                             2002008848

08  07  06  05  04  03  02          10  9  8  7  6  5  4  3  2  1

*To Gary Null and William Hare,*
*who have shown the way*

For a long time I sensed that there was much more to leadership than possessing a vast array of knowledge and learning a set of prescribed skills. I have seen too many individuals in leadership positions who, despite their knowledge and skill level, utterly fail to inspire and truly lead. I have learned from Null that we are certainly more than our conditioning or training. Each of us possesses ingenious qualities that work in harmony and manifest themselves uniquely. Our task is to discover these qualities, nurture them, and use them to become leaders in our own right.

Individuals who do not acknowledge the contributions of others, who are biased and unjust, who lack the steadfastness to make tough decisions, who don't really care about the needs of people, or who are closed-minded and uninspired too often occupy leadership positions in schools. Hare has affirmed the importance of going beyond cursory examination of credentials in selecting leaders and identifying individuals who possess noteworthy virtues that elevate them to excellence.

# Finding Your Leadership Style: A Guide for Educators

**Note: To use this book most effectively, please complete the surveys in Appendix A and Appendix B before reading the Introduction.**

# Preface

A couple of years ago, life took a turn that would forever change me—my father died. I was not the first child, of course, whose father had passed on. Moreover, I wasn't even a child—I was in my mid-40s. I am only now reminded of Mark Twain's quip about a child who realizes belatedly how intelligent and worthy his father was.

After observing the mandatory period of mourning according to my Judaic tradition, I knew I had to get away. It didn't matter where I went. Although I had hoped to secure the next available flight out of Newark and head to Arizona with its magnificent and inspiring panoramic desert, reality prevailed. I could not go anywhere that would cause me to miss necessary family and professional obligations in the ensuing days. I settled for a drive in my car.

I drove for a couple of hours and found myself in the Catskills. After driving up a deserted country road, I parked my car along a grassy embankment. The evening was cool and the stars shone brightly. Getting out of the car, I noticed a clearing in the trees ahead. Without thinking, I lay down in the clearing and felt the fallen leaves of early winter crackle beneath the weight of my body. I stared above and through a break in the trees.

Oblivious to the crawling insects and the sounds of barking dogs in the distance, I became absorbed in my surroundings. I breathed effortlessly and was filled with a sense of tranquility that had so far eluded me. How many others before me had experienced the beauty and splendor of this panorama? Why had I previously been so absorbed in my life and my work that I hadn't taken a moment to experience the grandeur of this view and the peace it provided?

Within a relatively short time (although a sense of timelessness overcame me that evening in the Catskills), my thoughts achieved a level of clarity heretofore lacking. Contemplating both the passing of my father and my own middle age, I began to examine certain personal accomplishments and goals. I asked myself, "Who am I? Am I using my talents in the best way possible?" It seems strange for someone approaching 50 to ask these fundamental and obvious questions, but I think many people begin to look at their lives differently at various stages, especially after major life events.

Satisfied and energized, I headed home. I had not discovered profound truths or insights, but I was roused by the moment, encouraged to begin examining my life as never before. That night, I slept comfortably knowing that my brief excursion was well spent. The very next morning I began an introspective journey from which this book is an outgrowth.

The story, however, was not over. Two experiences following this drive to the Catskills significantly affected me. As an editorial board member for a journal in educational foundations, I received a book to review written by a noted British educational philosopher named William Hare. Hare identified "virtues" he felt we should look for in teachers entering the profession. His work was illuminating and provocative. Later that week at my local Barnes & Noble bookstore, I came across *Who Are You, Really? Understanding Your Life's Energy*, written by Gary Null, a nationally renowned investigative reporter. I scanned the text and bought a copy. When I got home and started reading, I couldn't put the book down. I finished all 200 pages in a few hours.

*Finding Your Leadership Style: A Guide for Educators* was inspired by the convergence of these new insights about "qualities" and "virtues" and by my recent experience in the Catskills. It acknowledges the work of Hare and Null, but extends their concepts to provide a new perspective on educational leadership, an area neither author discusses. Hence, this work translates their theories into practice, much the way Madeline Hunter translated Benjamin Bloom's theoretical work into practical materials for teachers and administrators. Although much of what I say applies to any form of leadership, the emphasis in this book is on leadership in schools. The examples I give are drawn from work in schools.

This book was written for prospective and practicing school supervisors, administrators, teachers, and other educational leaders. Based in part on the work of Gary Null, this book encourages educational leaders to assess their personal style of leadership in relation to their ability to provide leadership in schools and districts. Seven distinct leadership qualities are discussed and practical examples culled from the experience of educational leaders. Included are practical strategies for actualizing a particular leadership quality, as well as strategies for effectively dealing and working with different leaders. The book also discusses seven different "universal" virtues (excellences) that educational leaders should possess, regardless of their "natural leadership quality"; these are gleaned from the work of William Hare. *Finding Your Leadership Style: A Guide for Educators* has implications for the kinds of leaders we should look for and can assist current leaders in assessing their own capacity to lead effectively.

After an introduction of the theme of the work, Part One outlines and details the seven leadership qualities, providing examples and relevant information. Part Two does the same for the seven virtues. Part Three pulls together the information from Parts One and Two by offering suggestions and strategies for actualizing your leadership quality, enhancing the universal virtues, and offering practical information for school leaders.

*Finding Your Leadership Style: A Guide for Educators* emphasizes individual talents and qualities as essential for effective leadership. A theoretical understanding of the systems and processes that influence individual behavior and form the foundation for educational leadership are certainly important (Sergiovanni, 2000). Although good educational leaders appreciate the complex dialectical relationship that exists between systems and individuals, this book refocuses attention to the more vital role of the individual leader.

The book presents an approach to leadership often missing in discussions about leadership. Leadership is a shared responsibility. It capitalizes on the unique qualities of all educational stakeholders who have specific attributes that can contribute to educational excellence. Everyone can lead to some extent in some situation, although it is true that all leaders are not alike. The text guides you to a better understanding of your leadership abilities and can help you to enhance interaction with others in and out of the workplace. *Finding Your Leadership Style* allows you to hone seven different leadership virtues, no matter what leadership quality you possess. By the end of the book, you will have a better sense of who you really are vis-à-vis your leadership potential and capacity.

This information also affords you a better sense of how best to use the leadership talents of others. If schools are to improve, we must tap the leadership qualities of the many as well as identify prospective leaders who possess important leadership virtues. That is why leadership is conceived and viewed as an inclusive activity. Teachers are vital leaders without whom school improvement will remain an elusive goal. The major premise of this book is that all educators are leaders in their own right. A successful leadership team is one that identifies individuals with the requisite qualities and virtues and matches them to a particular situation or project.

**Complete the surveys in Appendixes A and B
before reading the Introduction and the rest of the book.**

*You are a very special person
become what you are.*

—Archbishop Desmond M. Tutu

# Acknowledgments

I especially wish to acknowledge the contributions of the following people who have helped me bring this book to fruition. Gary Null and William Hare inspired me to examine school leadership in new and exciting ways. Kolene F. Granger, superintendent of Washington County School District in Utah, field tested the surveys and suggested a creative and useful way to arrange the survey items. Gerry Melnick, Osborne Abbey, Mark Goldberg, Bernie Flashberg, and Jeffrey Shurack helped me brainstorm ways to translate theories into practical examples, while the dedicated educators on my e-mail listserv shared their leadership ideas and experiences. Special appreciation to hundreds of former students and others who took the surveys and shared their reactions and thoughts that helped develop and improve my ideas.

I particularly want to thank Stephanie Selice, who believed that my insights into school leadership would have wide appeal. Although I have published eight previous books, I always wanted to publish with ASCD, the premier educational association in the world. Thanks to Darcie Russell for her expert work and suggestions that led to a manuscript that flowed smoothly.

I have been privileged to work with many dynamics, adaptives, and creatives who personify the essential virtues of effective leadership. Finally, to the reader, I challenge you to identify your leadership style, become the person you really are, pursue a fulfilling professional life, and achieve excellence in your chosen endeavors.

# Introduction

R oberta Rodriguez, principal of Boynton High School in an affluent suburb of Chicago, is the keynote speaker at the Parent-
Teacher Association's annual dinner. A dynamic, energetic visionary,
Rodriguez challenges the audience to adopt her "vision for a bright new
future for students at Boynton High" by voting for the new technology
bond issue, which she has spearheaded. "Our children deserve the
best," proclaims Rodriguez. "Our curricula must be and will be revised
to accommodate the ever-increasing technological demands of our
global economy. We can do no less." The audience breaks into a spontaneous, thunderous round of applause.

Orderly, autonomous, and highly principled, Roy Henderson, vice
principal in Margate Central District in Florida, plans for the upcoming multicultural festival at Waynebrook Middle School. Henderson
meticulously works out the logistics of the day's proceedings while sitting at his desk at 6:00 a.m. Making phone calls to local distributors,
scheduling classes for the three assemblies, and organizing a calendar of
the day's events are only a few of his chores on this bright Monday
morning.

Georgina Urbay, 5th grade teacher in Union Township, New Jersey,
always seems to find a different way of presenting information to her
students. Asked by her supervisor to conduct a workshop on creative
lesson planning to fellow teachers, Urbay accepts, albeit reluctantly.
Teachers respect her ability to remain sensitive to the individual needs
of students while at the same time developing "ingenious ways of taking a math or science idea, for example, and presenting the concept in
five different ways."

**Focus Questions**

1. Describe how these leaders differ.

_____

_____

_____

_____

_____

2. What do they have in common?

_____

_____

_____

_____

Each of the three vignettes depicts an individual who contributes to the school in different ways. Each is talented in a different way. Each is a leader. Roberta Rodriguez is clearly a take-charge dynamic visionary who can marshal forces to effect needed school reform. Roy Henderson is a fastidious, diligent, and highly competent administrator capable of planning for every contingency. While Georgina Urbay has neither the natural charisma of Rodriguez nor the steadfastness to details of Henderson, her creativity commands the respect and admiration of her students and colleagues.

Which description best represents you? In other words, which style of leadership (embodied by Rodriguez, Henderson, or Urbay) best matches your style of leadership? Describe how your style is similar or different. If your style does not match one of these leadership styles, identify someone who does closely match your style. Describe and explain.

_____

_____

_____

_____

_____

_____

_____

The fact that each of us has unique qualities and abilities is not new. As a professor who prepares future educational leaders, I always wonder if any teacher who enrolls in our supervisory certification program could become an effective educational leader. The question is, "Are leaders naturally gifted or can they be 'made'?" Null's Natural Life Energy theory is a groundbreaking tool for understanding our natural attributes. The implications for preparing and selecting future educational leaders are striking. To better direct Null's thesis to the work we do in schools, I've applied his theory to what I call "Natural Leadership Qualities (N.L.Q.)," while maintaining the integrity of his theory's major postulates.

Null defines seven distinct energies; I've adapted these energies to "qualities." Everyone manifests a particular quality. We feel most comfortable when we use and live by that quality. Part One of this book addresses the types of people who exhibit these qualities.

- Dynamic Aggressives—visionaries; the smallest percentage of the population
- Dynamic Assertives—the change agents, reformers, iconoclasts
- Dynamic Supportives—the nurturing helpers
- Adaptive Aggressives—individuals who aggressively pursue a goal
- Adaptive Assertives—excellent organizers

- Adaptive Supportives—trustworthy, loyal, hard workers; most of the people you'll ever meet
- Creative Assertives—visionary and artistic individuals

In the first eight chapters, we examine each leadership quality by defining its essential characteristics and by providing school examples of how the quality manifests itself in different people. The examples are offered to help you envision how the qualities appear and are applied in real life situations.

## Natural Leadership Qualities

We have natural qualities and attributes that make us unique and that drive or motivate us. How we react in a particular situation or crisis is determined by these natural qualities. Although many of us possess a constellation of attributes in differing amounts, we fall back on that dominant attribute or personality trait that comes most naturally to us in times of crisis or need.

A district, beset by warring factions, may hire a superintendent to articulate a community vision in which all vested interests can reach consensus. Yet, although the superintendent is managerially competent, she may not have the natural dynamic and charismatic qualities to bridge disparate viewpoints and factions. We must, according to the N.L.Q. theory, consider the match between the natural leadership quality and the task that needs to be accomplished. Not everyone has the same potential to bring a divided community or district to consensus. The superintendent, while competent and able to do many important things, may not be a good match for the needs of this district at that time.

What can we say about these leadership attributes or qualities in general? On one end of the spectrum, an individual may demonstrate charisma that can naturally influence or attract other people. On the other end of the quality spectrum are people who have no need to stand out. Rather, their expertise is in their ability to adapt well to any situation and to work diligently to accomplish their objectives. Each quality has its own resonance, strengths, and weaknesses.

## Primary Quality Types

Three primary leadership types exist: the Dynamics, the Adaptives, and the Creatives (see Figure 1). Dynamic individuals possess a charismatic quality, a personal magnetism that enables them to inspire and lead others. Dynamics have an ability to see the larger picture, can articulate a vision for the future, and have a strong sense of ego (e.g., Margaret Thatcher, Bill Clinton, Nelson Mandela). Adaptives, in contrast, are not charismatic nor are they looking to change the broad scope of situations; their sense of ego is much less pronounced than the ego of a Dynamic. Creatives (e.g., William Shakespeare, John Lennon, and Maya Angelou) have a personal rhythm, awareness, and sensitivity that allow them to perceive the world differently and more imaginatively than Dynamics or Adaptives.

---

**Figure 1**
**Primary Quality Types**

Dynamics are highly charismatic individuals.

Adaptives adapt well to varied situations, although they are neither charismatic nor creative.

Creatives are imaginative or have artistic ability.

---

These three main quality types are distinct from one another. If you've met Dynamics, you are not likely to forget them. These people take center stage and attract others to them and their ideas; these qualities occur naturally. An Adaptive or Creative may act or appear charismatic, but this characteristic doesn't come naturally. The characteristics of each quality type occur naturally and without contrivance.

## Secondary Quality Types

According to N.L.Q. theory, the primary quality types have three further divisions. Some people are characteristically aggressive, some assertive, and some supportive (see Figure 2).

---

**Figure 2**
**Secondary Quality Types**

---

Aggressives can be characterized as highly opinionated or even contentious.

Assertives are often secure and confident.

Supportives usually exhibit an encouraging and affable nature.

---

Aggressives have a driving, forceful quality and tend to lead or want to dominate others. These are take-charge people. Have you ever served on a committee and noticed one individual who immediately engages the group forcefully? These individuals have a need to be center stage.

By contrast, some people sit back and listen. Although these people are not driven to take charge immediately, they are confident and willing to put forth their strong views on matters at the right moment.

Supportive individuals are not natural leaders and they are not usually the most eloquent speakers. They act best in assisting roles, and are basically nurturing, happy to help, and truly concerned about the welfare of others.

## Forming Seven Quality Types

According to Null (1996), the three primary qualities and three secondary qualities "are like strands that form the warp and woof of personality. . . . They weave together in certain patterns that produce the rich tapestry" (p. 4) of seven N.L.Q. types. All of us, of course, possess a degree of each quality. At times, we can all demonstrate creativity, assertiveness, and even dynamism. Again, the point is that each of us has a dominant natural quality. When we operate within our quality type, we feel most comfortable and productive. It is who we really are when the curtains are drawn and we are alone.

The primary qualities combine with the secondary qualities to form seven distinct quality types (see Figure 3). According to Null, these seven types have been derived through empirical research and confirmed by thousands of individuals. I have administered the survey in Appendix A, have shared the N.L.Q. theory with hundreds of people, and can confirm Null's thesis. The chapters in Part One are devoted to explaining each quality type and their implications for leadership in schools.

**Figure 3**
**Seven Quality Types**

|  | **Dynamic** | **Adaptive** | **Creative** |
|---|---|---|---|
| **Aggressive** | Dynamic Aggressive (DAG) | Adaptive Aggressive (AAG) |  |
| **Assertive** | Dynamic Assertive (DAS) | Adaptive Assertive (AAS) | Creative Assertive (CAS) |
| **Supportive** | Dynamic Supportive (DS) | Adaptive Supportive (AS) |  |

Legend
D = Dynamic               AG = Aggressive
A = Adaptive              AS = Assertive
C = Creative               S = Supportive

## Points to Consider

• Most people exhibit a tendency toward one quality. In cases where individuals exhibit strong tendencies in more than one area, the qualities are likely complementary.

• We exhibit a particular quality as a natural consequence of who we are. In other words, these qualities manifest themselves uniquely and naturally. The particular quality comes easily and naturally to us. For instance, I may act dynamically, but if I am not naturally dynamic I may be perceived as just plain pushy. Each person should be allowed to express himself in a specific quality. For instance, parents who are both

Creative Assertives may have a child who naturally displays Adaptive Assertive tendencies. If these parents coerce the child to behave in a certain way based on their own qualities, the child will likely feel upset and become dysfunctional. An Adaptive Assertive child can never display the natural creativeness that Creative Assertives manifest.

• Each quality operates on a continuum, from high (up) to low (down). Dynamic Aggressives, for instance, may work to their potential and thereby achieve much good for an organization. If they are operating at the low end, however, they may exhibit some rather obnoxious and unethical behaviors and thus not contribute much to the organization. In fact, a person who operates at the low end of the Dynamic Aggressive spectrum (see Chapter 1) might cause the most harm to an organization.

## Leadership Virtues

Part Two of this book explains the virtues that every effective leader must and can possess. The virtues that Hare (1993) identifies are in essence independent of the qualities. In other words, each quality type should reflect these virtues at the optimal level. Still, as my research indicates, each virtue emanates from a particular quality type:
- Dynamic Aggressives—Courage
- Dynamic Assertives—Impartiality
- Dynamic Supportives—Empathy
- Adaptive Aggressives—Judgment
- Adaptive Assertives—Enthusiasm
- Adaptive Supportives—Humility
- Creative Assertives—Imagination

Again, although each quality has an associated virtue, all quality types have the capacity to demonstrate every virtue to some extent. In fact, the degree to which a particular quality manifests the virtue determines the success of that individual.

Please notice that "intelligence" or "competence" are not included as virtues, though they may have been included in your list from Survey

1 in Appendix B (pp. 197–198). These abilities are essential, but they are a given. So are descriptors such as "ethical" or "moral," which cannot, by the way, be easily defined and understood by all people. What may be ethical to one person may be scandalous to another. Still, the point is that someone who exemplifies these seven virtues will necessarily embody competence and intelligence, and will likely display ethical or moral behavior. Besides, ethics and moral conduct are largely included under the virtue of "judgment."

For each virtue listed, provide an example of how a specific leader exemplifies the virtue.

Courage: _____

_____

_____

Impartiality: _____

_____

_____

Empathy: _____

_____

_____

Judgment: _____

_____

_____

Enthusiasm: _____

_____

_____

Humility: _____

_____

_____

Imagination: _____

_____

_____

These are the virtues and qualities that leaders should possess. However, most educational leadership programs emphasize the knowledge and skills considered necessary to function effectively as a leader. Witness the curriculum guidelines for advanced programs in educational leadership put out by the National Council for the Accreditation of Teacher Education (NCATE). The guidelines list leadership standards that describe the knowledge and skills candidates need to receive certification. Thus, too much focus is on knowledge, techniques, and methods. Policymakers are often afraid that educators cannot make good judgments in selecting and appointing those who have desirable intellectual, moral, and personal qualities, therefore they may resort to requiring what they consider observable and measurable behaviors. Leadership, then, is assessed merely by the possession of information and skills. Yet careful observation reveals that leaders are successful because their qualities (capacities) are well matched to the leadership position they occupy, and because they exemplify special and necessary dispositions or virtues unique to educational leaders. These virtues, although definable and identifiable, are not easily quantified or measured. Hence, in the selection of educational leaders, these virtues are usually overlooked.

Jerome Garner graduated with top honors from a master's degree program at a state university in Michigan. According to his professors, Garner demonstrated competencies in organizational theory, action research, and instructional leadership. Consequently, Garner secured a position as vice principal at a local high school. Within a relatively brief period of time, however, he encountered several problems. Socially, Garner was ostracized by many of the teachers he supervised. They complained that Garner was overbearing and unwilling to allow teachers' input on curriculum decisions. This documented hubris was exacerbated by his lack of empathy. Teachers often complained that Garner was insensitive to their needs. For example, he only offered perfunctory condolences to one of his teachers when she returned to work after the death of her father. That same day, Garner berated the teacher publicly for not leaving adequate lesson plans for the substitute and proceeded to write a letter for the teacher's file. Although Garner was knowledgeable and skilled in several supervisory and administrative areas, he experienced much difficulty as an educational leader in the school. Despite corrective measures by the principal, Garner was soon dismissed.

## Focus Questions

1. What is a good leader?

_____

_____

2. What factors may have contributed to Garner's difficulties?

_____

_____

3. If you were the principal, how might you have assisted Garner?

_____

_____

4. What surprises you, if anything, about this story?

_____

_____

5. What are some conclusions about leadership that you can draw from the vignette?

_____

_____

_____

I readily acknowledge the importance of skills or techniques in educational leadership. Yet we tend to accentuate these practical domains of performance to the exclusion of dispositions that may be more important. Moreover, a person who possesses these dispositions can easily learn the requisite skills and techniques of leadership, but the converse is not always true. You may hire an educational leader who understands how to establish a budget, set priorities, and carry out a strategic plan. But this individual might, for example, exhibit unethical behaviors or demonstrate lack of empathy for colleagues and others.

The essential question we in the educational community must ask is, "What kind of leader do we want for a particular position?" Do we want leaders who are uninspired, dogmatic, unimaginative, and unethical, or do we want to attract leaders who personify humility, courage, impartiality, empathy, enthusiasm, and imagination? A major point made in this book is that we often fail to appreciate the practical significance of these qualities in our leaders.

Describe a leader who inspired you. What characteristics did the leader possess? Describe the extent to which you are able to emulate this leader.

_____

_____

_____

_____

_____

_____

_____

## Points to Consider

- Effective leaders exhibit all or most of the virtues.
- Leaders may display varying degrees or manifestations of each virtue.
- Although educational leaders may develop and improve their virtues, we must attract leaders who already possess these qualities.

# Understanding Leadership

Although the following statements are often made about leadership, they are wrong to some extent.

- Leadership is reserved for the few gifted individuals who have the capacity to lead.
- Leaders are dynamic and visionary.
- Leaders must be able to transform people and motivate them to higher ideals.
- Learning how to lead requires the study of great leaders such as Margaret Mead, Eleanor Roosevelt, Martin Luther King Jr., and Mahatma Gandhi.

- Preparing future leaders depends largely on effective programs that teach requisite knowledge and skills.
- Most leaders are "made" not "born."

In contrast, *Finding Your Leadership Style: A Guide for Educators* asserts the following fundamental observations.

- Leadership is not reserved for the select few. The capacity to lead resides in everyone to varying degrees; yet all leaders are not the same.
- All leaders do not have to exhibit charismatic or visionary capacities to perform effectively.
- That all leaders must do anything is a gross generalization and belies the fact that leaders have different capacities and purposes.
- Relying on the Great Model theory, which examines the lives and leadership styles of famous national leaders, only provides a glimpse into the kind of leadership necessary for most leaders. These dynamic leaders may provide inspiration and insight for dynamic individuals, but do not relate much to other types of leaders.
- We should attract individuals into leadership programs who exhibit and possess specific dispositions, or virtues. These traits or capacities cannot be learned or transmitted in college preparation programs, although they can be identified and improved.
- All people possess special capacities. These natural capacities are affected greatly by environmental factors. Although all people can operate to some degree dynamically or charismatically, these qualities manifest themselves in great and natural ways in only some people.

Thus the principles of this book can be summarized:

- Everyone can lead in some way to some degree in a given situation at some time
- All leaders are not the same. Leadership styles, personality, and traits vary greatly.
- No one way of leading is better than another. Each leader is talented in a different way.
- Effective leadership depends on the context. Matching the right leader to a particular situation is most important.

• Effective organizations need all types of leaders. Different leaders positioned strategically throughout a school or district can contribute greatly to organizational effectiveness.

*Leaders know themselves;*
*they know their strengths and nurture them.*

—WARREN BENNIS

# PART ONE

# Seven
# Quality Types
# of
# Educational Leaders

*Excellence exists in many dimensions. . . .*
*No one is or can be excellent in all these dimensions. . . .*

—LESTER C. THUROW

# 1
## Dynamic Aggressives

Wayne Stevens's mother will tell anyone who listens that her son was extroverted and gregarious from an early age. He craved attention as a youngster and wanted to be the center of all activities. As Stevens got older, he participated in school plays and was always ready to share his views and opinions. His teachers realized that Stevens had enormous potential as a speaker as well as an entrepreneur. "He always has his hand in some venture," relates his high school civics teacher. "Wayne is a risk-taker who clearly wants to succeed in all that he does. He also has the ability to sway others to his point of view. He has the 'gift of gab.'"

Although Stevens did not graduate with top honors, he was studious, diligent, and committed to succeeding. After graduating with a 3.21 GPA from a local state university, Stevens went into teaching. He enjoyed interacting with people. He especially liked the authority that went along with being a teacher. At a job interview, he shared that as a youngster of about 12 he used to write up math quizzes and administer them to his sister, four years his junior. Despite her protestations at these ordeals, Stevens explained not only the sense of power he felt in administering the quiz, but also his satisfaction in using a red pen to mark the questions his sister got wrong.

As a teacher, Stevens was well liked by his colleagues. He attended all school functions and was usually the center of all school parties. Wayne soon gained the respect of the school administration. "Mr. Stevens is clearly a natural leader; he will go far." Shortly after receiving tenure, Stevens was promoted to assistant principal in another school within the district; a few years later he was appointed principal in a neighboring district. After another principal position elsewhere, Stevens was appointed assistant superintendent of curriculum and instruction; within three years, he was named the district's new superintendent. Within 12 years, Wayne Stevens rose from an 8th grade teacher to a superintendent of schools.

## Focus Questions

1. What are the Dynamic Aggressive qualities that Wayne Stevens exhibited?

_____

_____

2. What factors may have contributed to Stevens's successes?

_____

_____

3. What are some of the strengths of such a leader? What do you think may be some weaknesses of such a leader?

_____

_____

_____

4. Do you know anyone who exhibited a similar "rise to stardom"? Describe.

_____

_____

_____

5. Draw some conclusions about Dynamic Aggressive leadership from the vignette.

_____

_____

6. What else would you need to know about Stevens to assess his leadership?

_____

_____


## Dynamic Aggressives: Charisma and Control

Dynamic Aggressive people are charismatic natural leaders of society. Think of presidents, prime ministers, generals, CEOs, superintendents—they are all Dynamic Aggressives. For these men and women, being goal-oriented and entrepreneurial and needing to control others come naturally. They enjoy power and, in fact, thrive on it. They are demanding to work for and have high expectations. Yet, on their down side, they have a hard time admitting mistakes and will often be silent rather than apologize for an error. Dynamic Aggressives are at the center of all activities, therefore they are not good listeners. If you would like to share a problem with them, for example, they are not likely to offer much assistance or even attend to your concerns. You'll get much more favorable results with Dynamic Supportives (see Chapter 3). Dynamic Aggressives are not necessarily the most highly educated people, but they are skillful orators. When they enter a room, they are immediately noticeable. You won't forget the experience of meeting a Dynamic Aggressive.

Dynamic Aggressives are intriguing; they are not an open book. They are contemplative and even mysterious at times. Other people are attracted to them and their ideas. Statistically, of all the quality groups, they make the most money. Hence, many wealthy people are Dynamic Aggressives. Their drive and ambition usually get them to the pinnacle of their organization.

Personal relationships may take a back seat to professional ambitions, especially when Dynamic Aggressives function at the low end of their quality. If involved in a relationship with a nondynamic individual, the Dynamic Aggressive dominates the relationship. Such relationships work as long as each partner acknowledges and is satisfied with the role. I think about my former teacher who is a Dynamic Aggressive and whose taste in art predominates the home he shares with his wife, an Adaptive Supportive (see Chapter 6). On the other hand, when two Dynamic Aggressives are involved in a relationship, watch out—a love-hate relationship is likely to prevail.

Based on what we know at this time, Dynamic Aggressives represent only 0.5 percent of the people you'll ever meet. As a quality group, they have the potential to do the most good for an organization (see Figure 1.1). Conversely, of all the quality groups, they can do the most

---

**Figure 1.1**
**Primary Characteristics of Dynamic Aggressives**

| | |
|---|---|
| Charismatic | Attract people; charming, magnetic, graceful |
| Natural leader | Guide and direct others |
| Goal-oriented | Keep the end in mind, the big picture |
| Entrepreneurial | Take risks; adventurous, courageous, exciting |
| Skillful orator | Speak well to large audiences |
| Diligent | Work hard; persistent, almost fanatical |
| Politically astute | Realize various constituencies and their vested interests |
| Extroverted | Enjoy being the center of conversation; loquacious |
| Domineering | Take charge; overbearing, authoritative |
| Big thinker | Set lofty goals; a visionary; see what no one else does |
| Intelligent | Formulate policies; crafty, discerning |
| Visionary | See the whole picture; imaginative, utopian |

harm. Adolf Hitler and Joseph Stalin could be considered Dynamic Aggressives functioning at the extreme low ends of the continuum (see Figure 1.2). Margaret Thatcher and Martin Luther King Jr. were also Dynamic Aggressives functioning toward the higher moral and ethical end of the continuum. Other Dynamic Aggressives that may come to mind include Franklin Roosevelt, Saddam Hussein, Genghis Khan, and Slobodan Milosovic.

---

**Figure 1.2**
**Dynamic Aggressive Continuum**

| Low end | High end |
|---|---|
| Impatient | Hard working |
| Unapologetic | Extroverted |
| Self-centered | Domineering |
| Demanding | Goal-oriented |
| Unforgiving | Charismatic |
| Highly critical | Articulate |
| Power hungry | Visionary |
| Controlling | Politically aware |
| Manipulative | Competitive |
| Can do the most evil | Can do the most good |

*Note:* Do not view this continuum only at its extremes. Individuals may exhibit these qualities in varying degrees.

---

Felix Fernandez, a state superintendent in the Midwest, is considered by all who know him as a top leader and policymaker. He is a competitive, action-oriented individual with the ability to motivate and lead others. He seeks to control people and influence the direction of education. Fernandez has risen to the top of his profession in the state, beginning as a teacher 20 years earlier. He is intelligent, outgoing, self-reliant, single-minded, and politically aware. His detractors, however, accuse him of sometimes acting in a stubborn and conceited manner.

According to a school superintendent who marveled at Fernandez's ability to "see the larger picture. . . . Felix has a 'gestalt' mind—everything is instantly seen. If you show him a lake, he'll visualize an ocean. If you show him a hill, he'll see beyond the obvious cluster of trees and immediately develop a forest of ideas. Once Felix has the vision, he easily rallies others behind him to carry forth and actualize the vision."

**Focus Questions**

1. What information indicates that Felix Fernandez is dynamically aggressive?

_____

_____

2. In general, is he functioning at the high or low end? Explain.

_____

_____

3. How might Fernandez behave if he were acting as a Dynamic Aggressive at the low end?

_____

_____

Al Johnson is a principal in an urban high school setting in a large district in a major city. He is acknowledged by many as a Dynamic Aggressive on the lower side. He is extremely demanding to work for and can push others to the limits of their endurance with his criticism. On one occasion, he chastised a secretary in front of several other people for submitting the wrong report to the district superintendent. Instead of apologizing and thus releasing tension, he is likely to sulk and is prone to anxiety attacks and depression. Strangely enough, many people find his aggressive behavior appealing. People, usually other quality types, are drawn to his powerful qualities.

**Focus Questions**

1. What information indicates that Al Johnson is functioning poorly?

_____

_____

2. Why do some people find his leadership style appealing?

_____

_____

3. How could you convince him to change?

_____

_____

## Women as Dynamic Aggressives

Dynamic Aggressives in schools have been predominantly men. Does this imply that women cannot display dynamic aggressiveness? Certainly not. However, young women who display such tendencies early in life are frequently conditioned by family, church, and school to downplay their dynamic and aggressive qualities. Consequently, these and other women are not afforded the same opportunity as men to actualize their leadership quality and are, at worst, coerced into assuming a new, more feminine role. Not allowed to exhibit their natural tendencies, these women are relegated to minor positions and responsibilities in the school organization. People prevented from manifesting their leadership qualities remain disappointed, anxious, and depressed, often with negative consequences to their health. Keeping these points in mind, consider the following questions.

1. Do you know any Dynamic Aggressive women? Have they actualized their leadership quality in your district or school? If so, how were they able to succeed?

\
\

2. Can you name five Dynamically Aggressive women political leaders in history?

\
\

3. What factors have inhibited some women from attaining positions of authority in the educational system?

\
\

4. How might we encourage and support Dynamically Aggressive women?

\
\

## Actualizing a Leadership Role

If you are a Dynamic Aggressive, you can best actualize your role as leader if you

• Focus on fundamental instructional issues. Although you are cognizant of the many political complexities that affect a school or district, focus on what really matters to students—instruction. Strive to encourage good pedagogy and teaching. Faculty and grade meetings should focus almost exclusively on instructional issues.

• Bring out the best in teachers. Effective Dynamically Aggressive leaders influence by identifying leadership qualities in others and providing appropriate support mechanisms, such as mentoring opportunities (Blasé & Kirby, 2000).

• Learn to acknowledge your mistakes. After you have made a decision about any educational matter, readily admit any errors you might have made and realize that others may have more viable solutions to school problems than you.

• Force yourself to listen carefully. Although you may have called the committee meeting and shared your vision with the participants, listen intently to the views of others. Take notes as they speak, use body language to indicate your attentiveness, and paraphrase their points.

• Support shared governance opportunities. Encourage others to aspire to democratic leadership by facilitating teacher empowerment and developing democratic structures and processes in a variety of school contexts, such as school-based leadership teams to revise curricula (Blasé, Blasé, Anderson, & Dungan, 1995).

• Focus on people, not the system. Although you tend to think big, don't forget to reward those individuals who work with you. Show gratitude and loyalty to them.

Of all the quality types, it is Dynamic Aggressives who have enormous impact on others. The decisions these educational leaders make affect many facets of our lives, from the remuneration we receive to curriculum revisions to job satisfaction. Dynamic Aggressives embody visionary leadership, and without them little would be accomplished in the organization. If you are a teacher and a Dynamic Aggressive, you will probably not remain a teacher for long.

# 2

# Dynamic Assertives

Sarah Thompson was precocious as a toddler. She not only walked and talked earlier than her siblings but she was more outgoing and, at times, rambunctious. As Thompson got older, she became more opinionated and boisterous than her classmates. "Sarah has a definite viewpoint and she is not reticent to offer her opinion," explained her 6th grade teacher during open school night. At times, her friends found her loquacious and mature beyond her years. Thompson was popular. She could figure out solutions to problems that were difficult for others. Thompson usually offered her advice on how best to complete a project. Her unique insights and perspectives were often highly regarded by her classmates and teachers alike. A nonconformist by nature, she did not readily accept the latest fashions in dress and music. Some of her friends were envious of her self-confidence. Although Thompson's high school guidance counselor described her as highly introspective and sensitive, Thompson viewed most situations critically. "Sarah could walk into almost any situation," explained her high school social studies teacher, "and immediately understand what was going on. She would immediately offer her viewpoint that included a list of suggestions for improvement." Her ability to intuit and creatively respond to any crisis attracted the attention of her college instructors. One of her college professors posited "Sarah's perceptiveness and keen insight are invaluable assets that will serve her well as a future scientist."

Although Thompson was uncertain of her future occupation, she did show much interest as a reporter for her college newspaper. An English major with honors, Thompson had already conducted several investigative reports that earned her accolades by her peers and professors. An editor at a local newspaper praised Thompson by describing her as persistent, sharp, and perspicacious—a natural reporter.

Thompson graduated college and attended a local school of journalism in the evenings. To earn money, she taught high school English during the day. Her wit, self-confidence, and highly energetic personality attracted the attention of her colleagues. Her principal remarked, "Sarah connects to the kids like no one I've seen in years. She reads her students and is able to offer them what they need emotionally and intellectually." The principal continued, "Too bad for us and them, I don't think she'll remain a teacher for very long." Possibly clairvoyant and certainly insightful himself, this high school principal was correct. After three years and having just earned tenure, Thompson gave up teaching for her first position as an investigative reporter for a local television station. Over the next several years, Thompson earned a reputation as a top-notch reporter. Although she loved reporting, Thompson found the thrill of different job experiences even more compelling. She went from reporting to directing to producing. One of her colleagues said it best: "Sarah is an iconoclast, a free-thinker, an innovator."

## Focus Questions

1. What are the Dynamic Assertive qualities that Thompson exhibited?

_____

_____

_____

2. What factors may have contributed to Thompson's successes?

_____

_____

_____

3. What are some of the strengths of such a leader? What do you think may be some weaknesses of such a leader?

_____

_____

4. Do you know anyone who exhibited a similar "life quality"? Describe.

_____

_____

5. Draw some conclusions about Dynamic Assertive leadership from the vignette.

_____

_____

6. What else would you need to know about Thompson to assess her leadership?

_____

_____

## Dynamic Assertives Are Nonconformists

Dynamic Assertive people are personally magnetic, spontaneous, intelligent, and are the creators of social change. They view situations and naturally plan ways of improving them. No societal or organizational change or improvement can occur without the leadership of someone who is dynamically assertive.

Dynamic Assertive people are charismatic nonconformists. While they may be trendsetters and revolutionaries, basically they are only looking to control their lives, not the lives of others. They know what they believe in and why, and what they don't believe in and why. They are conceptually creative and process oriented. They are generally not comfortable with single relationships as they are outgoing and yearn to learn and work with many different kinds of people. On their down side, they can be stubborn, they can overstep their bounds, and usually they have a hard time admitting mistakes. They also can be quite egotistic and controlling given each personality dimension (i.e., dynamic and assertive). Dynamic Assertive individuals will not maintain the status quo. They intuitively sense or read a situation and immediately consider ways of improving it. These societal or organizational reformers are exciting individuals. They are thinkers and doers. If you meet a Dynamic Assertive on the high end, you'll be impressed with their creative insights and the stamina they exhibit to actualize them.

Dynamic Assertives are instinctively distrustful of authority. Their strong individualistic drive can sometimes get them into trouble. In fact, Dynamically Aggressive leaders (e.g., Hitler) tend to initially and quickly eliminate Dynamic Assertives (e.g., Polish intelligentsia during the invasion of Poland at the start of World War II). Dynamic Assertives threaten the stability of the new regime because they tend to concoct ways of overthrowing the ruling government when it is dictatorial and immoral. In terms of school organizations, Dynamic Assertives may, for instance, threaten new superintendents who may want others to conform to their new policies. Transferring Dynamic Assertives who do not concur with the new policies is not uncommon. Dynamic Assertives naturally question standard operational procedures and seek news ways of doing things. They are not likely to do the same job twice in the same way. They are experimenters and risk takers. Their problem-solving skills set them apart from most other quality types.

People are attracted to Dynamic Assertives because they are, on their up side, generous, friendly, and hospitable people. They are also very spiritual; they have an existential sense of their being in relation to others and to the universe. Although they can certainly adhere to religious dogma, they tend to question ideas that others take for granted. They do not usually perform religious services or activities perfunctorily. They are also

31

introspective; in fact, of all the quality groups, they are the most so. Their ability to exhibit conceptual creativity comes from the fact that they give deep consideration to options and strategies. In addition, Dynamic Assertives have a strong personal sense of ethics. The end, for this quality group, does not justify the means.

Dynamic Assertives enjoy meeting and working with people; others are naturally attracted to them because of their dynamic qualities. Two Dynamic Assertives may get along well with each other; Dynamic Assertives may also interact easily with Dynamic Aggressives. The Dynamic Assertive will not be pushed around by the Dynamic Aggressive, as might another quality type. On the up side, their assertiveness keeps the relationship balanced and healthy. It is people who lack self-confidence and their own sense of security who feel threatened by Dynamic Assertives. Dynamic Assertives enjoy meeting and working with many different people. They realize that no one individual can fulfill their intellectual and social needs. Some people feel threatened by this tendency. Dynamic Assertives can feel suffocated by individuals who do not allow them to express their proclivity toward multiple social relations.

Based on current data (Glanz, 2002), Dynamic Assertives represent only about 5 percent of the people you'll ever meet (see Figure 2.1). As a quality group, they are high-powered leaders who have the potential to guide us to new vistas and possibilities. Mother Teresa, Mahatma Gandhi, Nelson Mandela, Eleanor Roosevelt, and Ralph Nader are examples of Dynamic Assertives who, at their best, functioned at the high ends of the continuum (see Figure 2.2).

Renaldo Jenkins, director for curriculum and instruction in an urban district in the East, is considered by all who know him as conceptually creative and quite daring. During his brief tenure as director, he has initiated three new curricular and instructional programs that have transformed the way the district conducts professional development for teachers and other professionals. Jenkins is highly sociable and well liked. He conducts lessons for teachers at any time and without apparent preparation. He appears to perform well at most tasks, and his talks are both inspirational and motivational. One teacher put it this way:

---

**Figure 2.1**
**Primary Characteristics of Dynamic Assertives**

| | |
|---|---|
| Change agents | Seek to improve a situation; facilitators, reformers |
| Personally magnetic | Realize people are attracted to their ideas; charismatic |
| Risk takers | Willing to confront a challenge; adventurous; explorers |
| Independent thinkers | Distrust authority; nonconformists; iconoclasts |
| Idealistic | Envision possibilities; optimistic, futuristic, confident |
| Introspective | Delve into the unknown; contemplative, serious |
| Spiritual illuminators | Sense the needs of others |
| Ethical illuminators | Tell the truth; honest (sometimes brutally so) |
| Spontaneous | Thrive on the moment; unpredictable |
| Exciting | Enjoy being on the move; involved in big projects |
| Powerhouses | Realize their "dynamic" and "assertive" qualities |

---

"Renaldo can do it all and he can get almost anyone to try a new idea. He shows the way."

According to the school superintendent who marveled at Jenkins's ability to "get things done, [Jenkins] sees a problem and devises numerous ways to solve it." Moreover, continued the superintendent, "he has the ability to marshal forces within the district and in schools to rally people around his innovative programs and practices. He is our catalyst for change in the district."

## Focus Questions

1. What information indicates that Renaldo Jenkins is a Dynamic Assertive?

---

2. In general, is he functioning at the high or low end? Explain.

_____

_____

3. How might Jenkins behave if he were acting as a Dynamic Assertive at the low end?

_____

_____

Angela Santos, a vice principal in a suburban elementary school on the West Coast, just completed her master's degree at a local university. She is proud of her accomplishments and publicizes them. Santos is

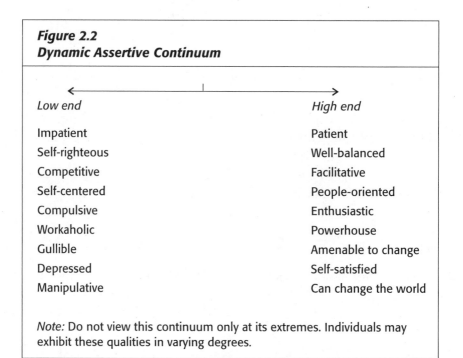

**Figure 2.2**
**Dynamic Assertive Continuum**

| Low end | High end |
| --- | --- |
| Impatient | Patient |
| Self-righteous | Well-balanced |
| Competitive | Facilitative |
| Self-centered | People-oriented |
| Compulsive | Enthusiastic |
| Workaholic | Powerhouse |
| Gullible | Amenable to change |
| Depressed | Self-satisfied |
| Manipulative | Can change the world |

*Note:* Do not view this continuum only at its extremes. Individuals may exhibit these qualities in varying degrees.

acknowledged by many as smart, quick-witted, and energetic. She rarely asks others for their opinions on curricular and instructional matters since she feels confident and knowledgeable. Her creative insights were crucial in terms of assisting the school to alter its traditional scheduling procedures. She researched and advocated a move to a limited block scheduling system that allowed teachers of reading and mathematics more time to help youngsters at risk to better prepare for the upcoming standardized tests. Her ascent from teacher to vice principal was rapid.

Although a gifted administrator, Santos intimidated many of the faculty. Her zealousness and compulsivity created a tense atmosphere for the teachers reporting to her. She continually pressured them to make certain that the students were well prepared for the reading test. Santos emphasized the use of test sophistication methods by constantly having students take practice tests, an approach not endorsed by her teachers. Although at times she could inspire them, her workaholic approach, impatience, and perfectionist nature increased stress levels among the teaching staff. Life around Santos was frenetic and fast paced, too much so for the teachers.

**Focus Questions**

1. What information indicates that Angela Santos is a Dynamic Assertive at the low end?

_____

_____

_____

2. What approach could Santos have used to avoid intimidating others?

_____

_____

_____

3. Does she remind you of anyone you know? Explain.

---

## Actualizing a Leadership Role

If you are a Dynamic Assertive, you can best actualize your role as leader if you

• Frame realistic goals for change. You are always ready to conceive and implement improvements to school and classroom. However, others may not share your eagerness for the changes you advocate. Be sure to establish practical instructional and curricular goals.

• Seek supporters or allies. Change is not likely to occur unless you identify reliable change agents who are like-minded and positioned to implement change (Hansen, Lifton, & Gant, 1999).

• Realize that neither centralization nor decentralization works. Both top-down and bottom-up strategies are necessary to effect district or school change. Use your talents to facilitate both processes (Fullan, 1997).

• As a change agent, you are a designer, not a crusader. Work as a leader to design learning processes whereby people are mentored, coached, and helped along the way. Older conceptions of school leadership make decision-making and problem-solving skills paramount. Although these skills are important, you are first and foremost a facilitator of change (Senge, 1990).

Of all the quality types, Dynamic Assertives are the great conceptualizers of change. These societal and organizational architects are responsible for innovative programs and practices. Without this quality group, little would change in our schools or districts; these are the reformers who show us new ways of organizing educational environments. If you are an educator and are dynamically assertive, nothing will remain the same as long as you are empowered to fulfill your natural leadership role.

# 3
## Dynamic Supportives

Did you ever meet someone whom you liked immediately? Well, almost everyone who meets Albert Chu likes him. Warm, outgoing, genuinely affable, Chu makes people feel at ease. He relates well to all people. According to his parents, he has always done so, and has always been ready to "lend a helping hand." As a high school student, Chu toyed with the idea of entering the healing profession in some way or perhaps going for a Ph.D. in psychology to become a therapist. His first love, though, was teaching. "I feel immense satisfaction from helping youngsters achieve their potential," Chu related to a close friend. Sincere, compassionate, and reliable, he attracted the attention of an assistant principal who interviewed him at the New York City Board of Education. "Mr. Chu," the report read, "is articulate, eager, and outgoing. He has all the qualities to make a fine teacher."

Chu was true to that report, and much more. He quickly gained a reputation in the school as a teacher who would do almost anything to support the needs of his students. He chaired various schoolwide committees, including the ones for the Student Awards Ceremony and Commencement. Chu was more successful than most teachers in helping resolve conflicts among students, and even those between teachers and students. He was often called on to offer conflict resolution sessions. Chu was considered by many a caring and fair teacher. No wonder he won the Teacher of the Year award for three out of his five years in the school. Although he changed schools three times during his 35-year career, he remained a teacher until his retirement. Honored many times, Chu informed the attendees at his retirement dinner that if he had to choose a career again, he would most definitely choose teaching. "Nothing, for me, could be as satisfying and rewarding than living up to the ideals of 'education.' The word comes from its Latin derivation meaning 'to draw out or to lead.' That's what we do—we help young minds to develop and assist young people to attain their potential. We don't always succeed, but when we do . . . there's nothing like it!"

**Focus Questions**

1. What are the Dynamic Supportive qualities Chu exhibited?

_____

_____

2. What factors may have contributed to Chu's successes?

_____

_____

3. What are some of the strengths of such a leader? What do you think may be some weaknesses of such a leader?

_____

_____

_____

4. Do you know anyone who exhibited a similar "life quality"? Describe.

_____

_____

_____

5. Draw some conclusions about Dynamic Supportive leadership from the vignette.

_____

_____

6. What else would you need to know about Chu to assess his leadership?

_____

_____

## Sincere Friends

Charismatic, warmhearted, sincere, reliable, humorous, compassionate, strong yet gentle—all these words can describe Dynamic Supportives. This quality type is typified in therapists, healers, clergy, guidance counselors, teachers, and communicators. They are independent, intuitive, and good at bringing people together, sometimes serving as bridges between Dynamics and Adaptives, and especially between Dynamic Aggressives and Dynamic Assertives. My guess is that a majority of the readers of this book, educational leaders of all sorts, are Dynamic Supportives because they really care about people above all.

Dynamic Supportives are the people who really care about you when they ask, "How are you doing?" They make the best friends because they listen well and offer assistance, even at great cost or trouble to themselves. They do so because they are driven to help others. It's what gives them the most satisfaction. And although they are willing to help almost anyone, they are no fools. Their "dynamic" quality makes them strong-willed, confident, and determined. They are charismatic, but they do not have the need to lead or control others. They can take charge of a situation but would rather not do so. Still, people are drawn to them; they have a presence.

Their willingness to help others sometimes, especially when on their down side, may affect their own well-being and health. When this occurs, they may experience lethargy, melancholy, or depression. On the down side, they have the potential to be the laziest of all the quality groups. Consequently, some Dynamic Supportives are procrastinators. One of the ways to identify people in this quality group is to look at their desk. Organization and cleanliness are not what drive them. Their desks have the "lived-in" look.

Dynamic Supportives, on their up side, are optimistic, easygoing, and selfless. In term of relationships, they accommodate everyone. Two Dynamic Supportives get along famously. They also get along with the previous two dynamic quality types. Dynamic Supportives share the "dynamic" quality, so they aren't intimidated by the others' aggressiveness or assertiveness. Put simply, Dynamic Supportives make the best friends.

Based on what we know from empirical research, this group represents from 15 to 20 percent of the people you'll ever meet (see Figures 3.1 and 3.2). As a quality type, they are genuine nurturing helpers who have the charm and inner strength to help us all. Can you name famous Dynamic Supportives? My guess is that you'll have a bit of difficulty. They don't usually make the headlines, but they stop to help you if your car is disabled. When you are new to the school or district, they are the ones who will offer genuine assistance. I am certain that those individuals who have risked their lives to rescue others are members of this quality group.

Janice Marselli has been a preschool and elementary teacher of children from a broad range of ethnic and socioeconomic backgrounds. She has long been committed to making schools more responsive to diversity among children. Speaking at the district's Annual Diversity Conference, she told her audience, "Teaching is a very complex and important job in today's world. We have the opportunity to make a difference with kids. We cannot, however, make a difference unless we demonstrate a deep love for all kids no matter who they are or where they come from. . . . We as teachers must act as champions of all children, especially the disenfranchised, in order to promote justice, equality, and opportunity. . . . I have had many high and low points in my career. I have had the pleasure over the years to work with many gifted and dedicated teachers. There is nothing like the teaching profession. . . . The bottom line is that I love kids, love teaching, and am very proud to be a teacher."

---

**Figure 3.1**
**Primary Characteristics of Dynamic Supportives**

| | |
|---|---|
| Charismatic | Personify a natural sense of presence |
| Warm hearted | Share; kind, considerate, compassionate |
| Sincere | Care; empathetic |
| Reliable | Trust others; your best friend in time of crisis |
| Humorous | Joke around; optimistic, funny, fun to be with |
| Articulate | Speak well; intelligent; good communicator |
| Emotional & spiritual | Sense the feelings of themselves and others |
| Easygoing | Enjoy play; joyful, noncompetitive |
| Strong-willed | Remain determined; confident; a strong ethical inner core |
| Gentle | Seek to reduce conflict; peaceful and amiable |

---

## Focus Questions

1. Although the information presented above does not provide many details about Marselli's personality, what information does indicate that Janice Marselli is a Dynamic Supportive?

---

2. How might Marselli behave if she were acting as a Dynamic Supportive at the low end?

_____

_____

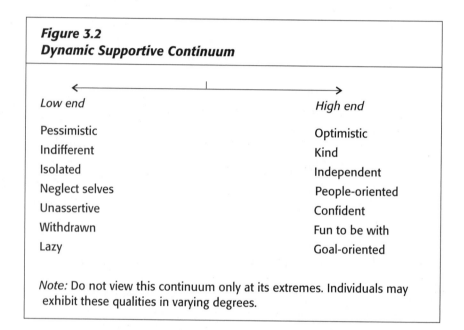

**Figure 3.2**
**Dynamic Supportive Continuum**

| Low end | High end |
|---|---|
| Pessimistic | Optimistic |
| Indifferent | Kind |
| Isolated | Independent |
| Neglect selves | People-oriented |
| Unassertive | Confident |
| Withdrawn | Fun to be with |
| Lazy | Goal-oriented |

*Note:* Do not view this continuum only at its extremes. Individuals may exhibit these qualities in varying degrees.

Francine Goldstein has been teaching for 10 years in a private school in Atlanta. She is generally warm, compassionate, and likable. Goldstein goes out of her way to help everyone, teachers and students alike. She works long hours and selflessly volunteers for any and all projects related to assisting the school and district. She rarely takes a day off, is continually barraged with requests for assistance, and has a hard time refusing anyone.

Early in November, her supervisor noticed that Goldstein "appears more harried than ever." Her attendance and curriculum reports are overdue. She even "appears disheveled and confused as she runs from class, to committee, back to class." Although she always experienced a weight problem, her weight seems to have gotten out of hand. Her supervisor advises her to "slow down, learn to say 'no,' and take a few days off." Goldstein seems perplexed as to why she feels more stressed than usual as of late: "I have always been able to balance my hectic lifestyle before!"

**Focus Questions**

1. Why is Francine Goldstein having difficulty balancing her professional and personal responsibilities?

_____

_____

2. Why do some Dynamic Supportives tend to ignore their own well being?

_____

_____

3. Do you know anyone like Francine Goldstein? Explain.

_____

_____

## Actualizing a Leadership Role

If you are a Dynamic Supportive, you can best actualize your role as leader if you

• Prioritize commitments. Although you are inundated with requests for assistance, learn not to accept every commitment before you have had time to consider it thoughtfully. Weekly, make a list of these requests for your time and prioritize them. Accept only those that you ranked in the top half of your list. For the others, call back and say you are already overcommitted with other projects. Don't be apologetic; be assertive. Although that is not part of your nature, it becomes easier with practice.

• Set aside time for yourself. You are always ready to help others, often at great personal expense. That's noble and very much needed, but you should realize that you are of no help to others if you don't care for yourself. Find time; don't plan too much. Be flexible and leave room for spontaneity. Take a mini-vacation in your office. Close your eyes and recall a wonderful, relaxed time you had on one of your vacations (Brownstein, 1999).

• Consider assuming small to mid-sized leadership positions. You probably don't have a drive to lead or direct others; you'd rather help people. However, you are talented and people are attracted to you. You can rally people around an idea. Use your interpersonal skills to humanize the school bureaucracy. As a Dynamic Supportive, you would make a good mid-level supervisor, such as an assistant principal, supervisor of instruction and curriculum, or principal.

• Serve as a buffer to the school bureaucracy. You are people-sensitive. Many people cannot confront the monolithic "steel monster" we call the "board of education." Frustrated, and treated sometimes without compassion, people often walk away from the school board or district offices with a distasteful experience. You can serve to mitigate such negative feelings. Treating people with dignity, respect, and caring comes easy to you. You represent the very best schools have to offer.

Dynamic Supportives are the most sensitive to the needs of other people of all the quality types. They feel most fulfilled in the helping professions. Their gentle charisma is a great asset to themselves and to others. Because Dynamic Supportives are often great conversationalists, they make people feel comfortable around them. Without this quality group, schools and classrooms would be places with a dearth of humanity, caring, and empathy.

# 4

## Adaptive Aggressives

At 7:55 a.m., Tim Hardy walks briskly through the corridor of the district office in search of the superintendent. An emergency has arisen that requires her immediate attention. After briefing the superintendent, Hardy is paged to return to his office to confront an irate parent. On his way, he meets several principals complaining about local construction projects interfering with school bus arrivals and departures. Hardy hurriedly assures them that he will attend to the matter later in the day. As he enters his office, his secretary hands him the District Improvement Plan document that needs revision before final submittal to the state. Glancing at the document, he half-heartedly listens to the parent's complaint about one of the district's principals and assures the parent that he will look into the matter. Within a few minutes of the parent's departure, Hardy is called into the superintendent's office. "Tim," explains the superintendent, "we have a contractual problem brewing among the teachers in the district related to hall duty and patrols. I want you to . . ." Hardy rushes out of the office to make some urgent calls. He advises the principal about whom the parent complained earlier to assent to the parent's request in order "to make this issue go away." "Just tell her what she wants to hear," he advises, "and later we can do what we want." Hardy then meets with his staff and issues directives for the day. The time is now 9:35 a.m. and the day has just begun.

Tim Hardy is not in the least fazed by the frenetic pace of this morning. In fact, he craves this fast-paced working environment. "Even when things are relatively calm," explains his secretary, "Tim can't sit still. He's always looking for action." Hardy has been employed in three different positions at five different locations during his 16 years in the system. He is very comfortable making job changes. On the job, he adeptly negotiates one crisis after another. His resourcefulness to "get things done" has earned him a reputation as a doer.

## Focus Questions

1. What information indicates that Tim Hardy may have exhibited Adaptive Aggressive qualities?

_____

_____

2. What factors may have contributed to Hardy's successes?

_____

_____

3. What are some of the strengths of such a leader? What do you think may be some weaknesses? Are any of these evidenced in Tim Hardy's case?

_____

_____

_____

4. Draw some conclusions about Adaptive Aggressive leadership from the example.

_____

_____

_____

5. What else would you need to know about Hardy to assess his leadership?

_____

_____

## Hidden Power

Although not charismatic, Adaptive Aggressives are drawn to power-ful people and have the resourcefulness to work with them. They are socially aware, goal-oriented, survivor types, and are expert at finding their niche within the power structure and using it. Successful public relations people, as well as "behind-the-scenes operators," are often Adaptive Aggressives.

On the down side, they can be very secretive and exploitative. The ends, they might say, justify the means. They are bright opportunists who can get the job done. They often surround themselves with Dynamic Aggressives who articulate the vision so that they, as Adaptive Aggressives, can carry out the plan. Nothing would or could get done in an organization without the hard work and cunning of an Adaptive Aggressive. They lead by example.

In terms of personal life, personal relationships reflect their fast-paced and volatile nature. They aggressively pursue their interests. Adaptive Aggressives generally get what they want. Superficial and controlling on their down side, members of this quality group at their worst could take advantage of most other quality types (especially Adaptive Supportives, Creative Assertives, and even Dynamic Supportives). They develop firm relationships most frequently with Dynamic Aggressives and, to a lesser extent, with Dynamic Assertives. The latter quality groups can more easily monitor the aggressiveness of an Adaptive Aggressive than can most other groups. Dynamic Supportives, because they are so "nice," can be easily taken advantage of by an Adaptive Aggressive who is at the lower end of the quality continuum.

Based on current data, this group represents only about 10 percent of the people you'll meet. As a quality group, they are exciting opportunists whose self-interests dictate the choices they make and how they conduct themselves in personal and professional relationships. Since they adapt well to varied circumstances and situations and act aggressively in pursuing a goal, they make the best survivors. In fact, if you're stranded on an island, seek out a member of this quality group because she is best suited to getting you to safety. A Dynamic Aggressive may rally people to action, a Dynamic Assertive may develop a rescue plan, a Dynamic Supportive may comfort you during this time of crisis, but it is only the Adaptive Aggressive who can take that vision and plan and make something happen.

It's hard to name many famous people from this group (unless you know the names of the winners of the "Survivor" television series) because they usually work behind the scenes to make things happen. Adaptive Aggressive people usually pursue careers as lawyers, salespeople, and actors, and function well as advisors, managers, and mid- to upper-level supervisors (see Figures 4.1 and 4.2).

---

**Figure 4.1**
**Primary Characteristics of Adaptive Aggressives**

| | |
|---|---|
| Resourceful | Make the best of a situation; ingenious; survivors |
| Socially aware | Understand the dynamics of social situations |
| Self-assured | Think independently; confident, strong-willed |
| Exciting | Enjoy challenges; energetic |
| Success-oriented | Strive for success; highly motivated to succeed |

---

During her interview for a vice-principalship in an urban district in the Southwest, Teresa Carter was clear about who deserves her allegiance. "I, as assistant to the principal, see my role exactly in that way; to assist her to carry out her policies. Although I certainly will assume leadership in areas that have been delegated to me, I will work assiduously to ensure that Ms. Parker's policies are implemented." Victoria Parker desperately sought an individual who would unconditionally support her initiatives. Working in a school that was troubled academically, Parker knew she had tough times ahead. Carter seemed to be the answer to her dreams. Teresa Carter, in fact, was just the person this principal needed.

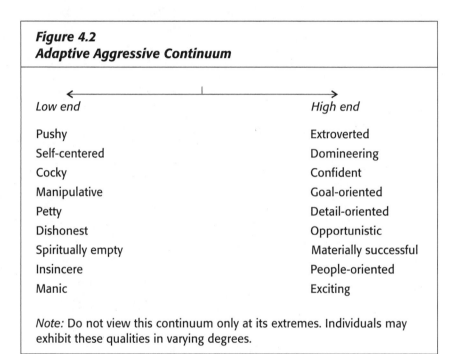

**Figure 4.2**
**Adaptive Aggressive Continuum**

| Low end | High end |
|---|---|
| Pushy | Extroverted |
| Self-centered | Domineering |
| Cocky | Confident |
| Manipulative | Goal-oriented |
| Petty | Detail-oriented |
| Dishonest | Opportunistic |
| Spiritually empty | Materially successful |
| Insincere | People-oriented |
| Manic | Exciting |

*Note:* Do not view this continuum only at its extremes. Individuals may exhibit these qualities in varying degrees.

Parker could always count on Carter's support for program initiatives. Carter proved to be a tireless worker. Eager, industrious, and resourceful, she found a way to get the job done despite programmatic and personnel obstacles that might have thwarted a lesser person—or a person of a different quality group. Parker, recounting some of the assets of her vice principal to the superintendent, explained, "Teresa transforms my vision into reality. She develops a plan of action, gathers faculty and staff support, attends to all logistical and administrative considerations, and most important, stubbornly pursues the vision to fruition. I don't know how she does it and I don't know what I would do without her."

## Focus Questions

1. What information above indicates that Teresa Carter is an Adaptive Aggressive?

_____

_____

2. In general, is she functioning at the high or low end? Explain.

_____

_____

3. How might Carter behave if she were acting as an Adaptive Aggressive at the low end?

_____

_____

Don Nastasi is director of personnel for a large urban district in South Florida. He is a self-assured pragmatist who has a reputation as a firm manager. Accountable directly to the superintendent of schools, his responsibilities include developing a recruiting, training, and retention plan for minority teachers in the district. Previous administrations had not hired sufficient numbers of educators from underrepresented groups. Committed to affirmative action and fervent in his belief in increasing minority representation among teachers and administrators in the district, Nastasi coaxed potential applicants to apply for positions in his district by offering generous salaries and benefits. Although well intentioned, Nastasi employed some rather questionable strategies to hire minority group members. For instance, on more than one occasion, he purposely ignored applications from qualified majority applicants while expediting applications from minority group members.

After receiving several complaints, a state supervisor discovered Don's practices. The official submitted his report after intensive investigations and concluded that Nastasi's "deceit consisted not so much of out-and-out lying as it does of lying by omission, or of exaggeration or rationalization." True to the downside of his quality, Nastasi's secretive and manipulative actions contributed to the very injustices he so ardently tried to prevent. At his hearing, Nastasi tried to rationalize his behavior "for the larger good," and even at one point blamed others for his personal deficiencies.

**Focus Questions**

1. What motivated Don Nastasi to act deceitfully?

_____

_____

2. Can you provide instances where others behaved unethically? What motivates them to behave that way?

_____

_____

_____

3. What differentiates high-end and low-end behavior for Adaptive Aggressives?

_____

_____

_____

### Insight on Adaptive Aggressives

Some years ago, I injured my back in a sporting accident. When none of the doctors I visited, traditional or alternative, offered comfort, a friend suggested I call a famous doctor in New York City who had been the physician to the New York Giants football team. I called for an appointment but, despite my gentle protestations about the pain I was in, could not get an appointment for two and a half months. The next year, a good friend of mine severely injured his knee. He, too, visited many doctors to no avail. I suggested he call the same renowned New York physician, but I warned my friend that the physician was very busy. My friend immediately called and the secretary informed him that no appointment would be available for three months. "What?" my friend shouted, "how dare you treat me that way! I am in pain! I demand to see the doctor. Is my knee worth any less than anyone else's?" He continued his tirade for some time. Shocked, yet proud of my friend's persistence (I could never have spoken that way), I was even more incredulous when he hung up the phone with an appointment for the very next day!

Well, that's the difference between an Adaptive Aggressive (my friend) and myself (an Adaptive Assertive). You'll learn about my quality in the next chapter.

## Actualizing a Leadership Role

If you are an Adaptive Aggressive, you can best actualize your role as leader if you

• Understand that the "means" are more important than the "end." Certainly some people judge you by your results. However important results are, you must realize that how you go about accomplishing them demonstrates your level of integrity. Raising test scores, for instance, is only important to the extent that students are engaged in meaningful learning activities and that teachers are providing instructionally sound pedagogy.

• Build allies. Although you, as an Adaptive Aggressive, are hard working and lead by example, you try too often to go it alone. Learn to build alliances through consensus building in order to support initiatives and programs. These practices will result in greater school-based implementation (Fullan, 1997).

• Maintain high ideals and a moral purpose. Appreciate the moral-ethical implications of your work in schools as you creatively synthesize the actions of others. In doing so, you will learn to affirm self-efficacy and to value individuality (Sergiovanni, 1992).

• Realize your context expertise. As an "Adaptive" leadership quality type, you have the natural capacity to understand and work well in multiple contexts (urban, suburban, multicultural, and global). You should also realize your ability to develop positive interactions in multiple communities (families, communities, and agencies). Continue to demonstrate a commitment to specific knowledge, understanding, and skills needed for relating to and taking account of these contexts. Also, appreciate all aspects of cultural diversity among students and community (Nieto, 1996).

Adaptive Aggressives, of all the leadership quality types, are the most resourceful and potentially powerful. They are bright and they are open to opportunities. They are often fearless and, most important, they make things happen. Without this quality group, little would be accomplished in the organization—Adaptive Aggressives have the unique ability to transform ideas into action.

# 5

## Adaptive Assertives

Zina McDonald arrives at her office at 7:00 a.m. each morning. She enjoys the quiet hour and 15 minutes before yard duty. She's able to review her e-mail messages, read her mail, and prioritize the day's activities. As one of three assistant principals in a large urban elementary school in Brooklyn, New York, McDonald is in charge of grades 4 and 5 in this K–5 school of 1,350 students. The school is beset with the usual social and economic difficulties that characterize similar inner-city schools. Lack of parental involvement, high rates of transfer, and inexperienced personnel are some of the prominent problems. Most of her day is spent on two major responsibilities: yard and lunch duties and dealing with disciplinary cases or hearings. Despite formidable challenges, McDonald has maintained an optimistic, dedicated approach to her work.

McDonald's colleagues view her as diligent, highly organized, and committed. Many teachers realize that she runs the school. The principal is widely known as a politician who tries to raise money from local and state nontraditional sources to support school initiatives. According to one teacher, "He does a good job in what he does, but he doesn't attend to the day-to-day operations of running the school. Zina, the most experienced AP, runs the school." McDonald is a stickler for details. She enjoys arranging schedules, coordinating cultural events, and organizing all the school's curricular programs. Parents and teachers like her because she is personable and dependable. She doesn't crave public attention. McDonald gains enormous satisfaction from doing her job in the best way she knows. Her greatest satisfaction comes from seeing meticulous plans implemented and having the school running smoothly.

## Focus Questions

1. What are the Adaptive Assertive qualities McDonald exhibited?

_____

_____

2. What factors may have contributed to McDonald's successes?

_____

_____

3. What are some of the strengths of such a leader? What do you think may be some weaknesses?

_____

_____

4. Do you know anyone like Zina McDonald? Describe.

_____

_____

_____

5. Draw some conclusions about Adaptive Assertive leadership from the example.

_____

_____

_____

6. What else would you need to know about McDonald to assess her leadership?

_____

_____

## Practical Leaders

Adaptive Assertive people are not necessarily charismatic, but they do have the kind of practical leadership skills that make them good supervisors, managers, and principals. They are solid, dependable, hard workers, and highly responsible. Adaptive Assertives are highly organized people, who tend to be neat and family oriented. They tend to the details of a job, and they are usually less imaginative than other types.

Adaptive Assertives prefer order and stability. They strive to achieve equilibrium. They have difficulty working in a chaotic environment and, on their down side, can get easily frustrated when their desires are not attainable. Still, they are persistent and motivated to keep trying. They are strong-willed, smart, and pragmatic. Department heads, chairs, principals and their assistants, and other supervisors are often members of this disciplined and idealistic group of people.

Adaptive Assertives don't usually stand out. They work behind the scenes in a self-effacing manner. They are highly principled and civic-minded individuals. On their up side, they are excellent workers and you can count on them in times of crisis. On their down side, they can exhibit compulsive and intolerant behavior.

In their personal life, members of this group could develop positive relationships with most other groups. However, the two groups who may clash with them are Dynamic Supportives and, especially, Creative Assertives. This latter group, as we will discover in Chapter 7, are almost the antithesis of Adaptive Assertives. The desire of Adaptive Assertives to control their environment can drive a Creative Assertive up the proverbial wall. Dynamic Supportives, especially at the low end, often encounter difficulties with Adaptive Assertives. Procrastination and laziness are not well received by an Adaptive Assertive. Their intolerance for such behavior can cause many an argument.

Based on what we know, this group represents about 15 percent of the population (see Figures 5.1 and 5.2). They are the most idealistic of the groups and value stability. Adaptive Assertives are punctual, persistent, thrifty, honest, and diligent. You probably cannot name any famous people from this quality group because they are not flashy and have no desire to call attention to themselves.

---

**Figure 5.1**
**Primary Characteristics of Adaptive Assertives**

| | |
|---|---|
| Organized | Plan well; neat, ordered, stable |
| Diligent | Focus on details; persistent |
| Civic and family-oriented | Follow the status quo |
| Dependable | Remain loyal; predictable, consistent |
| Principled | Believe in traditional values; honest |
| Diligent | Work hard; persistent, almost fanatical |

---

José Santiago, curriculum director for a suburban school district in Atlanta, Georgia, is considered by all who know him as one of the most fulfilled, functional individuals in the office. "José is a nice guy, quiet, reliable, hard-working, and a good planner," according to his fellow supervisors. According to the superintendent, "José has the ability to suggest changes in the curriculum, develop a detailed, well-researched proposal, and implement the revisions in a timely, efficient manner." Santiago readily admits that he doesn't have the inclination to reform systems, but he certainly can recommend reforms within his area of specialization.

On a personal note, Santiago is fit and trim. He exercises regularly and strives for self-improvement by taking vitamins. He belongs to a local health club. Married with three children, Santiago enjoys his spare time, albeit limited, with his family. Although not gregarious, he has a few friends outside work whom he has known since childhood.

**Figure 5.2**
**Adaptive Assertive Continuum**

←————————————|————————————→

| Low end | High end |
|---|---|
| Compulsive | Conscientious |
| Intolerant | Fulfilled |
| Unimaginative | Predictable |
| Uncaring | Dependable |
| Unrealistic | Pragmatic |
| Conceited | Smart |
| Anal | Punctual |
| Neurotic | Disciplined |

*Note:* Do not view this continuum only at its extremes. Individuals may exhibit these qualities in varying degrees.

### Focus Questions

1. What information above indicates that José Santiago is an Adaptive Assertive? In general, is he functioning at the high or low end? Explain.

_____

_____

_____


2. How might Santiago behave if he were acting as an Adaptive Assertive at the low end?

_____

_____

_____

James Monahan is a principal in a suburban middle school setting in a small district in Louisiana. He is stickler for every jot and iota inscribed in the Board of Education's rules and regulations. He abides by all standard operational procedures and expects all his teachers to do likewise. Although a practical leader, Monahan is often intolerant of others. He arrives at school on time every day and gets irritated when faculty are tardy. He has on more than one occasion chastised a teacher for not following prescribed procedures and adhering to Board protocols.

Not particularly warm and personable, Monahan prefers formal salutations when greeting his teachers. Dedicated to his job, he is first to arrive in the morning and last to leave. The chatter in the teacher's cafeteria is that "Mr. Monahan better 'get a life.'" He is known throughout the district for his long-winded memoranda detailing every exigency for almost every circumstance—from procedures during fire drills to lesson plan formats. Yet a fellow principal praised him, "Mr. Monahan runs an efficient school."

## Focus Questions

1. Why is James Monahan so attuned to details?

_____

_____

2. Is it possible to expect someone to act friendly, even if they are not naturally warm and friendly?

_____

_____

3. Do you know someone like Monahan? Give an example and explain her behavior.

_____

_____

## Actualizing a Leadership Role

If you are an Adaptive Assertive, you can best actualize your role as leader if you

• Realize the importance and value of systemic change. Change at the broader level does not come naturally to you. Although you prefer to work on things within your circle of influence, accept the larger views of others that seek macroscopic, systemic reform to the system. Acknowledge current research that demonstrates the need for both bottom-up and top-down strategies (Fullan, 1997).

• Learn to tolerate chaos and to go with the flow at times. Although you prefer an orderly, predictable work environment, you should realize the value of organized chaos. Confusion and uncertainty inspire some individuals to learn better and to work better. Also, appreciate the fact that you cannot control everything. To attempt to control everything only increases the levels of anxiety and stress around you. Understand emotionally that there is no way to control the world, but you can control the way you react to events (Lewin, 1993).

• Focus on instructional leadership. You are good at conducting research, compiling reports, collating data, and writing proposals and papers. Although these activities are important, remember to attend to urgent concerns. Attention to your role as instructional leader is paramount to having a positive effect on teaching and learning. Engage teachers in instructional dialogue and meaningful supervision (not evaluation) activities. Get out of your office into the classrooms and save the report writing for down times and after school (Sullivan & Glanz, 2000).

• Strive to achieve consensus and delegate authority. You tend to think you can do it all, and in many cases you can because you are competent and successful in most ventures. Still, learn the importance of involving others in meaningful decisions. Establish and coordinate school-based decision-making councils and committees. Also, designate others to assume responsibility for important tasks that you really cannot address. Selecting, for instance, other Adaptive Assertives (e.g., teachers) and Adaptive Supportives (next chapter) for such tasks can be a good idea (Hansen, Lifton, & Gant, 1999).

Adaptive Assertives may not have natural charisma or attract much attention, but, of all the quality types, they have an enormous capacity for planning, organizing, and coordinating events. These are the people who develop the plans for survival and escape from a deserted island. Adaptive Assertives are essential to maximize the effectiveness of any educational organization. Placed appropriately, they can contribute to the smooth and efficient operation of any school or district.

# 6

## Adaptive Supportives

Sherin Bariro, a recently certified teacher in the Boston public schools, spends a lot of time with her students during her planning periods and after school. She always wanted to teach. Her mother was a teacher; in fact, she comes from a family of teachers. Bariro realizes that teachers can act as an adult in students' lives with whom they have a stable, reliable, and nurturing relationship. "Why do I teach?" She responds simply yet profoundly, "It's the way I am."

According to her supervisor, Bariro is quiet, compassionate, and dependable. Her supervisor says that Bariro "goes well beyond curriculum and classroom management to reach her students. She makes herself personally available." One of her colleagues comments, "Sherin is the kind of person you'll never notice in a crowd. Yet, behind that unpretentious exterior lies a deeply sensitive, good person."

Bariro became involved in the Adopt-A-Classroom program. Hearing about the program from a friend in Florida, Bariro decided to use her spare time to solicit $500 donations from community stores, companies, and individuals to adopt classrooms at her school. The money goes to classes in need.

"It enriches our classroom environment," praises teacher Dawn Torre. "It's enhanced [student] learning and it's made [education] more interesting and fun for the students. They have access to things they didn't have before." In less than six months, Bariro solicited nearly $3,500. "In her quiet, unassuming manner, Sherin makes a difference," exclaims her principal. "She asks for no acknowledgement; in fact, she shies away from public recognition. In my book, she's a star."

**Focus Questions**

1. What are the Adaptive Supportive qualities that Bariro exhibited?

_____

_____

2. What are some of the strengths of such a leader? What do you think may be some weaknesses?

_____

_____

3. Draw some conclusions about Adaptive Supportive leadership from the example.

_____

_____

4. What else would you need to know about Bariro to assess her leadership?

_____

_____

## Trustworthy Supporters

Adaptive Supportive people make up the majority of the population; they are the nonglamorous supporters of the status quo and society works because of them. Adaptive Supportives are trustworthy, charitable, and good citizens. They trust authority and are, at times, afraid of change. They are functional, dependable workers.

Can Adaptive Supportives serve as leaders? Well, not in the same way as other quality types. They lack the dynamism and the potential to influence that Dynamic Aggressives and Assertives have. They even lack the charisma of a Dynamic Supportive, although they share the supportive quality with them. Although Adaptive Supportives share the adaptive quality of Adaptive Aggressives, they lack aggressiveness; they also lack the assertiveness of Adaptive Assertives.

So what kind of leadership qualities do they possess? Don't forget that all people can lead to some degree in some situations. Yet all leaders are not the same. Each has different abilities and skills. The critical idea is how best to use each quality. Adaptive Supportives do not assert leadership on their own. They must be empowered, encouraged, and guided to do so by other quality types. They respond best to requests made by Dynamic Supportives (because they share the supportive quality). However, they accede to the wishes of other Dynamics, Aggressives, and Assertives.

When given direction and encouragement, Adaptive Supportives can use their easygoing, charitable nature to provide the personal kind of leadership needed in certain situations. As intelligent, caring, humorous, and loyal individuals, they engender the trust in others. Others follow their lead because Adaptive Supportives are down to earth, nonpolitical, and not at all manipulative. Despite these advantages, their capacity to lead, compared with that of all the other quality types, is the most limited. In most situations, therefore, they are followers.

In terms of personal life, Adaptive Supportives form strong and enduring personal relationships early on and tend to stay in those relationships. They do well with others like themselves and also do quite well with Dynamic Supportives. If they are associated with other Dynamic quality types, the relationship cannot be an equal one because the Dynamics dominate the relationship. As long as the Adaptive Supportive consents, a relationship with a highly functioning Dynamic may be successful. A poor match is an Adaptive Supportive with an Adaptive Aggressive.

According to current data, Adaptive Supportives represent almost 40 percent of the people you'll meet (see Figures 6.1 and 6.2).

---

**Figure 6.1**
**Primary Characteristics of Adaptive Supportives**

| | |
|---|---|
| Supporting of status quo | Seek stability; conformist |
| Trustworthy | Rely on authorities; dependable |
| Charitable | Care for others; empathetic; activist |
| Good citizens | Trust authority; law-abiding |
| Hard working | Take job and responsibilities seriously |
| Traditional values | Establish a belief system |
| Consensus building | Work to avoid conflicts |

---

I am certain you have met many Adaptive Supportives. Describe one such individual. What evidence can you provide that indicates this person is an Adaptive Supportive? Does the description parallel your experiences with such people? In your estimation, can such people assume leadership positions? Explain why or why not.

_____

_____

_____

_____

_____

_____

_____

_____

_____

Babu Sprinivasin is a 5th grade teacher in Lincoln Elementary School in the Southwest. Unassuming, dedicated, and friendly to faculty and student, Sprinivasin works hard to prepare his students for the upcoming standardized state reading assessments. Students look up to him because he is perceived as honest and nonjudgmental. They feel comfortable going to him for advice, even on personal matters. "I can talk to Mr. Sprinivasin because he never prejudges or criticizes me. He listens and, most of all, he cares about me. He goes out of his way to ask me how I'm doing."

His peers also respect Sprinivasin because he is a consensus builder. Teachers know they can always go to him for advice and to serve as a buffer between warring factions. "He is calm and neutral. He has no hidden agenda. People feel comfortable to speak with him. They know he will be fair and forthright." Another colleague put it this way: "Babu

---

**Figure 6.2**
**Adaptive Supportive Continuum**

←—————————————|—————————————→

| Low end | High end |
|---|---|
| Inflexible | Hard-working |
| Introverted | Easy going |
| Conciliatory | Charitable |
| Corny, dull | Humorous |
| Depressed | Happy |
| Judgmental | Friendly |
| Too trusting | Loyal |
| Fear change | Honor their beliefs |
| Need to be accepted | Seek small-scale leadership |

*Note:* Do not view this continuum only at its extremes. Individuals may exhibit these qualities in varying degrees.

---

rarely volunteers for leadership; yet, when approached he is always friendly and eager to assist any way he can. He leads by example. He cares. More leaders can learn from his easygoing style."

**Focus Questions**

1. What information above indicates that Babu Sprinivasin is an Adaptive Supportive?

_____

_____

2. In general, is he functioning at the high or low end? Explain.

_____

_____

3. What do you think his colleague meant when he said that Sprinivasin "leads by example" and that other "leaders can learn from his easygoing style"?

_____

_____

4. How might Sprinivasin behave if he were acting as an Adaptive Supportive at the low end?

_____

_____

Ann Harewood worked her way up from paraprofessional, to assistant teacher, to licensed regularly appointed teacher in a suburban district in Tennessee. She is the first member of her family to graduate from college. She worked hard to achieve her current position. "I never thought I would make it. My family was in dire poverty. I am so fortunate."

Harewood is a happy, self-satisfied individual. Although she is well liked by her students, Harewood doesn't contribute to the school beyond her specified duties. When once asked to coordinate a grade-school play, she refused, saying she preferred not to take responsibility. On another occasion, when given the opportunity to transfer to a higher academically performing class, she also refused stating that she would rather work with the more academically challenged pupils. Her supervisor observes that Harewood rarely changes a lesson and does not seem to be open to ideas and innovative practices.

**Focus Questions**

1. Why is Ann Harewood so unwilling to take a risk?

_____

_____

2. Can Harewood change her preferences? Explain.

_____

_____

3. How have you related to people like Harewood?

_____

_____

## Actualizing a Leadership Role

If you are an Adaptive Supportive, you can best actualize your role as leader if you

• Serve as a role model by encouraging collegiality. There are always several individuals within the system who try to adhere to the old industrial model—an obedient workforce predisposed to following orders from above. But you know that schools are too complex for such isolated decision making. You realize the importance of allowing others to assume more responsibility and to participate fully in shared decision making. Since you are more people-oriented than most quality types, you can encourage others to work closely with their colleagues on instructional, curricular, and administrative matters. Avoiding impersonal or bureaucratic relationships in favor of encouraging personal relationships within a learning community can be your foremost contribution (Goodlad & McMannon, 1997).

• Bring out the best in others. Your ability to influence and empower others lies deep within you. You understand the power of praise, of maintaining high expectations of others, of involving others in decision making, of granting professional autonomy, and of leading by supporting others. It is leading by example that helps you to empower others (Blasé & Kirby, 2000).

• Create and communicate core values. You are influenced by fundamental values that serve as an anchor for the entire organization. Be sure to articulate and share your values with others. Communicate that high-quality instruction is the primary focus for achieving student success. Also communicate that the power to make decisions should be distributed throughout the organization, using support, information, and resources. And finally, communicate that diversity should be valued and evident in schools and districts (Patterson, 1993).

Adaptive Supportives are the functional workers who can, when empowered, serve as leaders within specific spheres of influence. Since they make up the majority of people, nothing in the organization can occur without their willing involvement. If you are a teacher and an Adaptive Supportive, you are likely to remain a teacher for a long time. Yet do not make the mistake of thinking that you are "only a teacher, and what can you do?" You are the backbone of the school organization, and your involvement is integral to its success.

# 7
# Creative Assertives

Karem Mohammed is working late one hot summer evening. It's now 1:00 a.m. as he labors over the project he has been working on for several months. He is compelled to complete this project before school resumes. Suddenly Mohammed stops working and decides to fly to Nevada, 300 miles away. He gathers a few belongings, packs his laptop, and heads for the airport. When he lands, he takes a cab to the nearest hotel, rests a bit, and then takes another cab to the desert. The cab drops him off on an old country road and he begins to walk. Enjoying the beautiful natural surroundings, Mohammed climbs a small hill from the top of which he can see the panoramic horizon. He sits, gazes, and contemplates.

After nearly an hour, he takes out the laptop and types feverishly. By the time he looks up, he notices the battery is running low; Mohammed hurriedly saves the material to the hard drive and to a diskette. Feeling satisfied, he grins and ambles back to the nearest gas station where he hails a cab back to the hotel.

Mohammed is a gifted English teacher who volunteered to write a script for the school's centennial celebration. Realizing his proclivity to delay projects, Mohammed started writing in early May with his first draft deadline set at the end of August. The program committee is set to review the script in early September.

Mohammed is also a visionary. Naturally creative and imaginative, he is a writer who adopts some odd working habits. "Hey," he tells his close friend (a Dynamic Assertive), "it works for me. I am more productive when I venture out on my own and do what normal people wouldn't." Back at school, Mohammed has the sensitivity and caring to work closely with his students to encourage their ideas and perspectives. Although at times immersed in his own projects and not driven to lead others, Mohammed readily assumes leadership roles in productions of school plays, school or district commemorations, and even at state fairs. According to his principal, "Karem inspires us by example. His enthusiasm and love for his work encourages his students and colleagues to participate in the meaningful curricular and extracurricular projects that are so important to our school."

**Focus Questions**

1. What are the Creative Assertive qualities that Mohammed exhibited?

_____

_____

2. What factors may have contributed to Mohammed's successes?

_____

_____

3. What are some of the strengths of such a leader? What do you think may be some weaknesses?

_____

_____

4. Draw some conclusions about Creative Assertive leadership from the example.

_____

_____

5. What else would you need to know about Mohammed to assess his leadership?

_____

_____

_____

_____

## Right-Brain Problem Solvers

Creative Assertive people are not dynamic or charismatic (think of Woody Allen), but display heightened sensitivity and perceptual ability. They are absorbed in their work, reflective, self-sufficient, creative, sometimes volatile, and visionary; they question life and themselves. Creative Assertive people view the world differently than most other quality types and are generally artists, designers, and novelists; think Picasso, Shakespeare, and Rembrandt. They are right-brain thinkers— Adaptive Assertives are left-brain thinkers. In school life, Creative Assertives have bright, fresh ideas about partial or whole school reform and have the ability to creatively problem solve. Although they shy away from management positions, their insights and leadership are invaluable and make school life interesting.

In terms of personal life, Creative Assertives are gentle, caring, and sensitive people on their up side, and can develop meaningful relationships. Two Creative Assertives, for instance, make a great match. A Dynamic Assertive and a Creative Assertive are also wonderful together. As mentioned earlier, Creative Assertives have great difficulties with the organized, neat lifestyle and compulsivity of an Adaptive Assertive. Creative Assertives, on their down side, experience great emotional volatility. Their mood swings and unpredictable behavior can be quite disconcerting and require enormous patience from their partners.

According to current data, this group represents about 5 to 10 percent of the people you'll meet (see Figures 7.1 and 7.2). As a quality

---

**Figure 7.1**
**Primary Characteristics of Creative Assertives**

| | |
|---|---|
| Heightened sensitivity | Care; thoughtful, perceptive |
| Absorbed | Reflect; contemplative, introspective |
| Self-sufficient | Think independently; avant-garde |
| Visionary | Look beyond the ordinary; imaginative |
| Emotional | Feel for others; emotionally intelligent |
| Unpredictable | Think outside the box; complicated |
| Driven | Compelled to create |

---

group, they are free, expressive, and exciting to be around on their up side. On their low side, they are irascible and volatile.

Maria Martinez, a director of curriculum in Texas, is considered to be one of the most innovative curriculum practitioners in the city. Her innovative alternative assessment practices have earned her local and state recognition. At a recent honors ceremony for Martinez, Superintendent Thompkins described her style of leadership, "Maria keeps her own hours. She may arrive at work at 1:00 p.m., but everyone who knows her realizes that she sets her own pace. She is self-motivated, highly energetic, will work round the clock when she needs to, and, most of all, inspires many teachers and other supervisors to examine their work in ways they never considered." Thompkins provides an example, "During one particular workshop, she led the group through a meditative exercise to stimulate their thinking out of the box. She asked them, 'Imagine you are a Martian, observing a classroom [yours] unbeknownst to the teacher. What would you see? Now, what suggestions might you [the Martian] make to the teacher [you] about conceiving new ways of teaching the subject matter?'

"I marveled," continued Thompkins, "how she was able to elicit such provocative ideas from people, whom I thought had no creative bone in their bodies. . . . Maria then followed up to help these teachers implement newfound ideas by visiting them in their classroom."

**Figure 7.2**
**Creative Assertive Continuum**

| Low end | High end |
|---------|----------|
| Forlorn | Caring |
| Isolated | Immersed |
| Brusque | Gentle |
| Self-centered | People-oriented |
| Depressed | Emotional |
| Highly critical | Expressive |
| Pessimistic | Optimistic |
| Craves acceptance | Confident |
| Inconsistent | Reliable |
| Vulnerable | Creative |

*Note:* Do not view this continuum only at its extremes. Individuals may exhibit these qualities in varying degrees.

## Focus Questions

1. What information indicates that Maria Martinez is a Creative Assertive?

_____

_____

_____

2. In general, is she functioning at the high or low end? Explain.

_____

_____

_____

3. How might Martinez behave if she were acting as a Creative Assertive at the low end?

_____

_____

Sopitu Soth arrived in the United States from Cambodia in the late 1970s. Despite a difficult life in his home country, he worked hard to become an ESL teacher in an urban district in Minnesota. Soth has a reputation in his school as a loner; he rarely participates in school social activities. Although he implements innovative teaching practices in his classroom (e.g., cooperative learning strategies and multiple intelligences-based projects), his behavior appears erratic to his supervisor. His supervisor comments, "Sometimes he seems as if he is walking in a dream, out of touch with what is occurring beyond his classroom. He rarely engages me in conversation. His apparent lack of self-confidence is disconcerting. I don't know how he manages to teach as enthusiastically as he does!"

Prone to fits of anger and pessimism, Soth's eccentricity and volatility have resulted in increased stress levels and forced him to take a two-month leave of absence. According to a colleague, however, when Soth comes out of a "'coma' . . . he is sociable, if not gregarious, and a very effective, creative educator."

## Focus Questions

1. What information indicates that Sopitu Soth is functioning on his low side?

_____

_____

_____

_____

2. Why do you think he exhibits mood and behavior shifts?

_____

_____

3. Can Creative Assertives function well on school committees? Explain.

_____

_____

## Actualizing a Leadership Role

If you are a Creative Assertive, you can best actualize your role as leader if you

• Help others to see alternatives to current practice. You have the ability to see possibilities in situations where others cannot. Articulate your vision for the way things could and should be by providing concrete examples; always understand that some people may need time to fully acknowledge your insights. Patience and perseverance are needed to rally others behind your vision.

• Develop a collective vision of where the school should be going. Projects that require your creative input might influence classroom practice, but it is also vital to use your talents as a leader to develop a collective vision for the school. You can do so by serving on a school-based leadership team if you are not in a position of authority (Starratt, 1996).

• Accentuate continuous learning for both students and educators. As an active learner, you realize that all learners have to be involved in the construction of their own knowledge. Reflective practice is a prime vehicle for an educator (Byrd & McIntyre, 1997). As Fullan (1997) explains, "Quality learning for all students depends on quality learning for all educators" (p. 5).

Creative Assertives, of all the quality types, are natural creators and doers. Although not inclined to manage or supervise, they are invaluable assets to schools or districts because they think imaginatively. Without this quality group, the school organization would be boring.

# 8

## Using Leadership Qualities Effectively

Chapters 1 through 7 introduce the seven different types of leadership qualities (see Figure 8.1). Each leadership quality has unique characteristics that determine the leadership abilities and strengths of the people who manifest that quality. The premise is that *all* people can lead, though talents and spheres of influence vary. Every successful school system enjoys success as a result of the collective talents of its leaders.

As mentioned in the earlier chapters, school systems are too complex for leadership to be reserved for a select few. Although these systems must have the leadership of a Dynamic Aggressive, they also need a full complement of educators, serving in different capacities, to effect any overall systemic changes. Thus school systems need the overarching insight of a Dynamic Assertive to jump-start whole school reform. In addition, they need the personal charisma of a Dynamic Supportive, the steadfastness of an Adaptive Aggressive, the organizational skills of an Adaptive Assertive, the devotion to sound values of an Adaptive Supportive, and the creative problem-solving ability of a Creative Assertive (see Figure 8.2, p. 81). These individuals exemplify the character qualities naturally; everyone's unique talents are needed for the improvement of schools or districts.

After reading these chapters, you understand the contributions that can be made by people from each quality. If you took the survey in Appendix A, you can identify your own natural leadership quality or qualities.

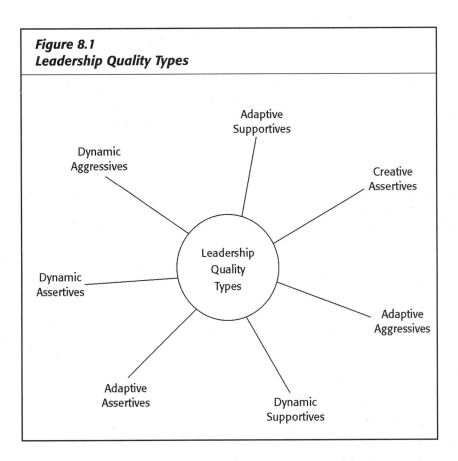

**Figure 8.1**
**Leadership Quality Types**

Adaptive
Supportives

Dynamic
Aggressives

Creative
Assertives

Dynamic
Assertives

Leadership
Quality
Types

Dynamic
Assertives

Adaptive
Aggressives

Adaptive
Assertives

Dynamic
Supportives

## Principles of N.L.Q. Theory

Here is a review of the fundamental principles underlying N.L.Q. (Natural Leadership Quality) theory and a guide to help you interpret the results of the leadership survey (Appendix A).

• The characteristics enumerated in this book for each of the seven qualities are generally positive ones. Yet each N.L.Q. possesses a high side and a low side, an up side and a down side. When we are functioning optimally within our N.L.Q., we are on the high side of our quality. At these times, we are fulfilled and are making a contribution to our school and district. However, each quality type may not function optimally all the time. Sometimes a dysfunctional characteristic such as laziness, unwillingness to change, and ill-advised stubbornness may be manifest.

• No one quality is best. You are who you are. Organizations need all quality types. Although the amount of talent can vary, everyone has what it takes to lead. A Dynamic Aggressive is not necessarily more talented than a comparable Creative Assertive. Each person has specific talents and can make unique and valuable contributions to the school organization.

• Each quality can teach and inspire others in significant ways. For example, we learn affinity for hard work from Dynamic Aggressives; sociability from Dynamic Assertives; warmth and friendliness from Dynamic Supportives; creativity and spontaneity from Creative Assertives; devotion to family values from Adaptive Supportives; organizational and time management skills from Adaptive Assertives; and propriety and seriousness from Adaptive Aggressives.

• Everyone can lead, yet not all leaders are equal. N.L.Q. theory affirms that all of us have the potential to lead under the right circumstances. Georgina Urbay (see the Introduction), a Creative Assertive, can certainly lead and inspire others toward creativity. Yet according to N.L.Q. theory, Urbay would not, and probably could not, achieve the lofty objectives that Roberta Rodriguez, a Dynamic Aggressive, was trying to accomplish for the entire district. Leadership is context-specific. Under special circumstances, a Creative Assertive or even an Adaptive Supportive can offer leadership. Other situations, however, might call for the particular dynamic leadership skills of a Dynamic Aggressive or Assertive.

## Survey Interpretation

Obviously, no survey can entirely encapsulate your leadership tendencies. Still, respondents overwhelmingly attest to the accuracy of the survey in Appendix A. In that leadership survey, you were asked questions to help determine your leadership quality. With that information in hand, please note the following guidelines when interpreting your results.

**Figure 8.2**
**Contributions from Each Natural Leadership Quality**

| | |
|---|---|
| Dynamic Aggressives (DAG) | Visionary |
| Dynamic Assertives (DAS) | Reforming |
| Dynamic Supportives (DS) | Collaborative |
| Adaptive Aggressives (AAG) | Persistent |
| Adaptive Assertives (AAS) | Organized |
| Adaptive Supportives (AS) | Moral |
| Creative Assertives (CAS) | Imaginative |

• The column on the answer sheet that has the most circles (as a result of the true responses), indicates the leadership quality that you manifest above all others. For instance, if you circled 7 out of 8 numbers in the column for Creative Assertive, and all other columns yielded smaller numbers of true responses, then you are a Creative Assertive. Most respondents have one quality that yields a clearly higher number. Note, however, the second-highest category. Was it even close to the highest? If it wasn't, then you are clearly the quality that scored the highest. On the other hand, if you had one or more categories that yielded almost as many "true" responses, you have strong inclinations for those leadership qualities.

• If you scored an equal number of "true" responses (e.g., 8/8 for Dynamic Supportive and 8/8 for Adaptive Assertive), then you manifest multiple leadership qualities simultaneously. That simply indicates very strong leanings in different styles. However, it is unlikely to have equally high scores in incompatible qualities. For example, if you scored equally high in the Creative Assertive category and the Adaptive Assertive category, then retake the survey. These are incompatible qualities, as are Dynamic Aggressives and Adaptive Supportives; Dynamic Assertives and Adaptive Supportives; and Adaptive Aggressives and Adaptive Supportives.

As you learn about your own leadership qualities, it's natural to wonder about the qualities exhibited by those close to you. You may find it interesting and enlightening to administer the survey to colleagues, friends, family members, and your partner. Do the results accurately reflect the natural qualities you've observed in those people?

Educational leaders must be prepared to deal with the political, economic, technological, and social realities of schooling. Educational institutions are too complex for the one-person approach to leadership. As we prepare future educational leaders, we need to identify those qualities in each person that can help us meet challenges. N.L.Q. theory allows us to identify, reaffirm, and understand leadership qualities that can enable leaders to successfully confront the plethora of challenges.

Schools require leadership qualities exhibited by Dynamic quality types, as well as those leadership qualities available from Adaptives and Creatives. No one person can personify all qualities. Successful school leadership demands that we identify leadership qualities unique to different individuals. The talents of each individual must be given expression within the school organization.

Ask yourself these questions: Which quality do I manifest most? What unique leadership contributions can I make to my school organization? Am I a good educational leader? How do I know? By answering these questions honestly, you have an informed basis for putting your talents to best use in your school or district.

# PART TWO

# Virtues All Educational Leaders Should Possess

*Character is what you are in the dark.*

—Dwight L. Moody

# 9

## Courage

Marigona Gashi never thought herself a courageous person. "I just plod along, an average person trying to do what's best for our students," she claims. A social studies supervisor for a large suburban district in Massachusetts, Gashi is noted for her commitment to ensuring that all students are challenged to think critically about historical events, rather than simply memorizing dates and facts. Her workshops on critical thinking have received wide acclaim by teachers across the district. According to one teacher, "Marigona is not only intelligent and articulate, someone you can respect for her knowledge and experience, but she is also sensitive to the varied ways people learn. Her attention to learning styles and the multiple intelligences theory are appreciated."

Arriving at work one Monday morning, Gashi was given a message to call Boris Speer, president of the school board. Gashi had only met Speer at various board functions, but everyone in the district recognized him as a Dynamically Aggressive individual. Aloof and self-confident, Speer had several worthwhile projects under his leadership. Gashi returned his call.

Speer told her that he wanted to speak with her about an urgent matter and asked if Gashi could meet him for lunch. To Gashi's surprise, Speer took her to one of the finest local restaurants. During their almost one-and-a-half-hour lunch, Speer dominated the conversation, reviewing his achievements and articulating his vision for the future. Although Gashi appreciated the scope of his projects on behalf of the district, she silently wondered why she had been asked to lunch. After all, she was in no way involved in district politics. Then the reason for the meeting became apparent.

"Ms. Gashi, my nephew has applied for the social studies teaching position in your area. Although he is a new graduate, he is intelligent and enthusiastic. He has the right stuff to become a great teacher. I'd appreciate it if you would consider him for the position." Gashi recognized the name as one of the applicants and assured Speer that his nephew would be given fair consideration along with all the other candidates. But this was not what Speer wanted to hear.

Sitting more erectly in his chair, he leaned closer to Gashi and said, "Let me be clearer, a bit more explicit—I'd really appreciate your help in this matter." He then abruptly asked for the check and escorted Gashi back to the office. Aghast at Speer's crassness, she didn't inform even her closest friends and colleagues about the incident. Over the next several days, Speer's called Gashi on unrelated matters a few times, which puzzled her because he had not called her before.

Gashi completed the interviews for the social studies position the following week; Speer's candidate was clearly inferior to other applicants. Gashi knew that the person filling the position had to replace her best and most experienced teacher. Although she knew which candidate deserved the job offer, she spent several days longer than she would ordinarily have done to consider the candidates. Finally, she made up her mind.

Although aware of the potential consequences, Gashi did not select Speer's nephew. The new candidate assumed his position, and she heard nothing further from Speer. However, when she applied, as she did every year, for release time to attend a national conference on social studies, she received a written note from the assistant superintendent denying her request. Outraged and confused, she confronted him, but he had only a flimsy excuse. Gashi was similarly refused release time for other events. In one instance, she had to use sick leave to attend a local workshop. Later still, when district funds were curtailed for her professional development projects, Gashi's indignation turned to anger and resentment as she realized the price of her action.

**Focus Questions**

1. What are the indicators that Gashi demonstrated courage?

_____

_____

2. What factors may have contributed to her courageousness?

_____

_____

3. What would you have done in a similar situation?

_____

_____

4. Why is courage so vital a virtue for an educational leader?

_____

_____

5. What are some other ways educational leaders can exemplify courageousness?

_____

_____

## Steadfast in Your Beliefs

What does it mean to be a courageous leader? The word "courage" conjures up military motifs such as heroic acts, daring exploits, and dramatic displays of fearlessness. What do bravery, gallantry, and valor have to do with educational leadership? Do school leaders really display inspiring acts of heroism? Why does a leader have to personify courage to be considered a good leader?

Although many forms of courage exist (e.g., physical, mental, or moral), the kind of courage necessary for educational leaders is the willingness to stand up for what they know to be right in the face of opposition. What is needed is the courage to speak out despite the constraining, formidable forces that serve to stifle individual initiative. These forces urge, if not compel, conformity to the status quo and are strong. To remain subservient to individuals in positions of power and authority or even to people who aggressively argue their position is execrable. Being courageous as a matter of principle should be valued and affirmed. By showing yourself to be principled, you are displaying immense strength of character. It is this strength of character that we call "courage." We need leaders who will gallantly assume responsibility for ensuring that the rights and dignities of others, especially the disenfranchised, are recognized and upheld. Speaking out against injustices such as unfair tracking placements, racist practices, and homophobic attitudes are just a few examples of courageous behaviors. The following examples of courage stand out in my memory.

> I coached boys' junior high school baseball for many years (although I teach at the high school). One year an event occurred that needed attention and discipline—and it probably cost us an undefeated season. My 7th and 8th grade baseball players went into the girls locker room after school (no girls were present) and did minor damage. I was the only one in the building and I could have ignored it. I didn't. I benched the offenders (most of the starters) and we lost the next game. But, I received great support from the parents. The easy thing to do would have been to ignore or assess a minor punishment and preserve our record. (Bernie Flashberg, Cranford High School, New Jersey, personal communication)

> I was on a committee to select a new vice principal for our school. The committee had decided to select the candidate

who earned unanimous approval. Everyone else was enthralled by a particular candidate, yet my gut reaction was that something was not right about the guy. The vote was cast and I was the only negative vote. The committee members drilled me for nearly an hour to change my mind. I was adamant. I don't think I was stubborn; I felt the candidate was morally deficient. Nothing he said led me to believe that; rather, it was the way he answered the questions. I could not convince others to share my view and the committee remained deadlocked. We reopened the search and eventually selected another person unanimously. Later we discovered that the original candidate had been charged with fraud, with the case pending during our interviews. I am glad I had the courage to withstand the pressure of my peers whom I greatly respect. (Jeffrey Shurack, New York City, personal communication)

These examples of courage are the manifest ones. Leaders also display courage in less visible ways. On a daily basis, they are expected to exhibit more subtle forms of courage: the courage to do what others prefer not to do, the courage to confront difficult and uncomfortable situations, the courage to remain steadfast in their beliefs.

Leaders may not exhibit physical bravery daily (e.g., confronting a knife-wielding assailant), but every day they have to affirm their beliefs about what is most educationally sound. Courage in leadership does not involve performing minor administrative tasks, filing reports, or reviewing teacher lesson plans. These are the necessary but perfunctory duties leaders may perform. Courage comes into play when one's beliefs and attitudes about teaching, learning, students, supervision, and schools are called into question. Remaining faithful to educational and moral principles is what courage is all about.

A courageous leader, therefore, should have a well-reasoned, articulated belief system that supports and affirms the rights and dignities of all learners, of all people. All leadership quality groups need a firm set of leadership beliefs to guide their behavior. In this sense, then, courage is integral to the effectiveness of a leader.

## Actualizing a Leadership Role

As an educational leader you can best actualize your role as a courageous leader if you

• Articulate your beliefs. Studies demonstrate that people with firm beliefs are more courageous than those who act impulsively. Critically examining your ideals and values and then forming a belief system can provide the bedrock upon which to rely when you are confronted with a crisis that threatens them (Osterman & Kottkamp, 1993).

• Role-play situations that require courage. As hokey as this suggestion may sound, acting out a response to a situation before it transpires can fortify you. Imagine, for instance, standing up to an irate parent who storms into your office and demands your time. This is admittedly a simple example for which courage may be needed, but nonetheless it's a good way to start. Close your eyes and imagine this parent entering your office. What can you say to her to communicate your desire that she call for an appointment in the future? Try to say something without sounding rude and disrespectful. You might say, "I'd like to see you, but this is a bad time. I must attend a meeting with a teacher. I will call you later to set up an appointment to discuss your concerns." If she insists on seeing you now, don't falter. Use the "broken-record" technique. Restate your position firmly while maintaining eye contact. "I understand that you want to speak with me, but this is not a good time." Once successful, by the way, you will gain the confidence to display similar degrees of courageousness (even more so) in the future. Recall what Aristotle once said: "We become brave by doing brave acts."

Why is courage such a vital virtue? Without courage, educational leaders become mere technicians, administrative guardians, and nothing more than custodians of the institution. Leading involves making the right decisions to benefit students, parents, and community. Schools are confronted by a panoply of demands that require educational leaders to hold fast to the beliefs that support student learning. The courage to stand up for what is right will safeguard the beliefs we hold as true.

Courage, then, is defined as the ability to stand behind one's principles, an ability that displays immense strength of character.

How can we ensure that prospective and current educational leaders are courageous? We should value courage and begin to identify the acts or behavior patterns of individuals who want to be or who are in leadership positions. There is no quick and easy survey to administer; anyone can answer the statements in the Appendix B survey dishonestly. The way to begin to assess courage is by asking and looking for instances in which leaders have demonstrated courage. That moves us a little closer toward understanding whether someone possesses it. The next step is to identify those individuals who articulate firmly held beliefs that affirm the values the institution of schooling holds in high esteem, values such as democracy, fraternity, and justice for all people. Only in this way can we hope to zero in on those leaders whose innate courage can keep our institutions strong.

*Courage is leadership affirmed.*

—Erik Erikson

# 10

## Impartiality

Alice Ota has been fighting bigotry as long as she can recall. A Japanese American, Ota remembers her parents' stories about being forced to live in U.S. internment camps during World War II. "My parents never held back anything," she explains. "They wanted to tell me about all they had experienced, including the intense hatred for the Japanese during that time. I am a stronger person today because of them."

For 22 years, Ota has taught at Renford Elementary School in Oklahoma. Originally, Ota recalls that her school "was relatively homogeneous. I remember . . . when [only] a few students from Japanese families registered for classes."

According to veteran teacher Mark Hamilton, "At first it was a novelty. It was something a little different and everybody rallied around the students." He continues, "Each year, however, was more and more diverse." The minority population in the school grew gradually yet steadily. About five years ago, Mark was walking the hallways of the elementary school during an annual multicultural celebration when he realized just how diverse the school had become. "Students were displaying personal artifacts from eight different Asian cultures," Mark recalled.

Of the 2,150 students in the school district, 31 percent are minorities. Asians are the largest group, making up about 28 percent of the student body. Latinos, African Americans, Native Americans, and Alaskan Natives account for less than 4 percent of the student body. Aside from an annual multicultural fair, few activities were developed by the school administrators to foster intergroup understanding and tolerance training. In fact, a few incidents of intolerance and bigotry were reported to the County Bias Crimes Unit. One of those was outside Ota's classroom, where someone had written with an indelible marker, "Chinks and gooks go home." Alice Ota was frustrated. She recalls how cruel students were to her growing up and didn't want what happened to her to happen to these children. She decided to make a difference.

With the permission of her principal, Ota called a meeting to discuss the increasing bias incidents in the school. She volunteered to chair a committee that would work with district officials, concerned parents, and the police. The Renford Prejudice Reduction and Tolerance Committee began spreading their message throughout the district. The immediate goal was to create a dialogue between students and their parents. "Our long-term goal is to create an institutional environment of understanding," said Fred Ford, father of a 6th grader. Workshops were conducted to help parents talk to their children about tolerance. "Some parents express prejudice at home and communicate it to their children," explained Ota.

The work of the committee spread across the district and more parents, teachers, and administrators got involved. Research projects were done, school and district fairs, along with town meetings, were held to discuss related issues of antibias education. "If you teach your children to accept differences, they grow up without resentment or hatred," said Ota during one workshop session. Activities, of course, also included students. Think tanks, advisory committees, and wide-scale classroom discussions fostered greater tolerance among students. One student said, "I've always thought intolerance comes from a lack of education. These projects helped educate us, and now we are going to help educate others." Students at nearby schools developed interschool tolerance fairs where students exchanged projects and art work. Terrence Kim used to hang out with only other Korean students. Today she is friends with kids from several cultures, and she says, "Who I am friends with isn't a problem for me."

## Focus Questions

1. What are the indicators that Ota demonstrated impartiality?

_____

_____

2. What factors may have contributed to her impartiality?

_____

_____

3. How do you think "impartiality" is defined in this chapter?

_____

_____

4. What are some other ways educational leaders can exemplify impartiality?

_____

_____

5. Why is impartiality so vital a virtue for an educational leader?

_____

_____

Impartial leaders can come from any background, in any form. The word "impartial" may conjure up images of umpires at baseball games or judges weighing evidence at trials. Whether an umpire or judge, these individuals make decisions by weighing evidence presented to them, considering the evidence within a prescribed set of rules, and rendering decisions. Although baseball umpires have to make instant decisions while judges benefit from deliberation, the judgments are presumed to be based on fair, unbiased assessments.

As educators, we need to ask ourselves the following questions: What does impartiality have to do with leadership? Is it possible for an educational leader to assume an impartial stance when dealing with complex issues involving students, parents, educators, and the community? Why does a leader have to personify impartiality to be considered a good leader?

Impartiality is defined in this context as behavior that is free from prejudice and bias—no individual is favored over another. Bias undermines leadership because it interferes with an impartial review of evidence and argument. If our approach is biased, we fail to do justice to those who rely on our judgment as leaders. If we are biased, we are inclined to accept some position or account more readily than another.

Take a situation in which a principal is confronted by a wealthy and well-known parent whose son is charged with a crime that warrants suspension from the school. The parent privately pleads with the principal for special consideration in this matter. It takes courage to withstand such requests, but what are the alternatives? Can committed educational leaders abrogate responsibility to treat all clients equitably and justly? By showing partiality to a child whose parent is prominent in the community, aren't we performing an injustice to another child whose parent is less prominent? Favoritism leads inevitably to corruption. To render an unbiased decision, educational leaders must be committed to assess fairly all relevant evidence while staying immune to the personal or social pressures.

Does impartiality mean we are neutral? Neutrality may indeed be difficult, if not impossible. No person can be prejudice-free. Our biases run deep. They are culturally and socially ingrained, reinforced by family and peer pressures. We are often oblivious to how they operate, how they shape what we see, and how we interpret meaning. As human beings, we are bound by our perspectives, our unique vantage points. Reality is seen and understood through the prism of our belief systems, which are based on assumptions gleaned from our experiences. Thus reality is dependent on our thinking patterns, belief systems, and mindsets. Our belief systems are connected to the language we use to communicate meanings that influence our actions and behaviors. How we think shapes the world in which we live. Learning to be impartial means we are cognizant of our biases, prejudices, and predispositions. Leaders *should* be impartial. When they know they are strongly committed to a viewpoint, leaders must compensate for bias by giving alternative views a fair hearing and representation.

Impartiality, however, is more than assuming a bias-free disposition. Although awareness is certainly critical, educational leaders are charged with the responsibility of taking action to combat prejudice, discrimination, hate, and injustice.

Good educational leaders understand the importance of maintaining a bias-free attitude that includes following a judicious and impartial review of relevant evidence in all cases and not simply proceeding from a partisan position and holding onto certain views dogmatically. Awareness of bias and the action to combat it is possible and necessary in our diverse, multiethnic, multiracial society. Everyone, despite leadership qualities, needs to understand personal prejudices and confront biases wherever and whenever they surface. Impartiality is integral to the effectiveness of a leader.

**Impartiality Activity**

Read the following story and, using only the facts as they appear in the story, answer the questions. (*Suggestion:* This exercise is best done when the story is read to you.)

## The City

It was hot and sticky in East Harlem. Tempers flared easily in the heat and humidity—it is the roughest time of the year in the city. A businessman had just turned off the lights in the store when a man who spoke with a strong accent appeared and demanded money. The owner hesitated, then opened a cash register. The contents of the cash register were scooped up, and the man sped away. A police officer was given details of the event very soon after it happened.

Answer each statement by marking it as True, False, or Unknown.

1. A man appeared after the owner had turned off his store lights. [T/F/U]

2. The robber spoke with a strong accent. [T/F/U]

3. It was summer when this incident occurred. [T/F/U]

4. The man who opened the cash register was the owner. [T/F/U]

5. The man who demanded money scooped up the contents of the cash register and ran away. [T/F/U]

6. A businessman had just turned off the lights when a man who spoke with a strong accent appeared in the store. [T/F/U]

7. Money from the cash register was scooped up by someone. [T/F/U]

8. The details of this event were promptly reported to a policeman. [T/F/U]

9. The owner scooped up the contents of the cash register and sped away. [T/F/U]

10. The following events occurred: someone demanded money; a cash register was opened; its contents were scooped up; and the man dashed out of the store. [T/F/U]

All ten statements are unknown. Each statement makes strong inferences about the facts in the story. Explore the distinction between inference and observation. We often make inferences automatically and unconsciously. This activity helps to reveal hidden inferences. All humans make lots of assumptions. What are our assumptions based on? Can educational leaders check their assumptions to avoid erroneous judgments? Impartial leaders can.

Now that the point has been made, explore the inferences you made with the explanations that follow.

1. We do not know for certain that the owner and businessman are the same person. If they are not, the owner might not be a man.

2. We don't know whether this was a robbery or someone demanding rent or strongly requesting payment for services or goods.

3. It can be hot and humid in late spring or early fall.

4. Again, we don't know if the owner was a man.

5. The owner could have been the one to scoop up the contents of the cash register. Does "sped away" necessarily mean ran away? What if the money were scooped up by our accented man who was on roller skates or was leaning out of his car at a drive-up window? Or what if this were a sidewalk sale, and the owner scooped up the cash register contents, then jumped in a waiting taxi and sped away?

6. We don't know if the man actually appeared in the store. He could have appeared at the door or at the window. He may not have entered the store.

7. We know there was something in the cash register, but we don't know if it was money. What if the cash register contained only food stamps? Vouchers? Coupons? Receipts? A gun?

8. We don't know if the police officer was a man. We don't know whether someone promptly reported this event or happened to mention it casually to a passerby who worked as a police officer.

9. It is possible that the owner scooped up the contents, but we don't know.

10. This is fine until we get to "dashed out of the store."

The exercise and answers are adapted and reprinted by permission of Joan V. Gallos from *An Instructor's Guide to Effective Teaching: Using Bolman and Deal's Reframing Organizations*. San Francisco: Jossey-Bass. (1991/1997; copyright © Joan V. Gallos). The exercise is excerpted and adapted from *Uncritical Inference Test*, copyright © 1982 by William V. Haney. Used by permission of William V. Haney. The test is available for classroom use from the International Society for General Semantics, Box 728, Concord, CA 94522 USA.

**Impartiality Activity**

The following quotation addresses the issues of equality and justice in the educational system.

Our system of education is fundamentally based on the rhetoric of equality and justice. Unfortunately, the reality is that there are social, economic, and political conditions that contribute toward, and help to legitimize, inequalities. Moreover, public schooling has perpetuated and reinforced social class, racial, and gender stratifications in a number of insidious ways. Inequalities are evident in each of the following ways: (1) unequal allocations of resources to different schools; (2) socially stratified arrangements through which subject matter is delivered; (3) low teacher expectations; (4) biased content of curricular materials; (5) patriarchal relations through authority patterns and staffing; and (6) differential distribution of knowledge by gender within classrooms. One of the most fundamental questions that needs continuous and vigilant attention is, How can we as educational leaders promote the ideals of justice, equality, and opportunity in our classrooms, schools, and communities?

With this quotation in mind, please answer the following questions.

1. What inequities and injustices have you witnessed or experienced in your school or district?

_____

_____

2. What does it mean to "promote justice, equality, and opportunity in our classrooms, schools, and communities"? Provide examples in which you have seen these ideals promoted.

_____

_____

3. Do you agree or disagree with the quotation? Explain.

_____

_____

4. What does the virtue of impartiality have to do with the notions expressed in the quotation?

_____

_____

5. Why is it important for educational leaders to champion these ideals?

_____

_____

## Actualizing a Leadership Role

As an educational leader, you can best actualize your role as an impartial leader if you

• Examine your biases. The word "prejudice," derived from the Latin noun _praejudicium_, originally meant precedent—a judgment based on previous decisions and experiences. Later, the word came to mean a judgment formed before examining and considering all the facts. It is not easy to say how much fact is required to justify a judgment. Prejudiced people say they have sufficiently considered all the facts to warrant a viewpoint. They may then relate negative experiences with groups such as Catholics, Jews, Irish, or Hispanics. Examining your biases presupposes the understanding that everyone is prejudiced to some degree; that is, they sometimes make prejudgments about people and in certain situations. "Are all or most women poor drivers?" "Do all or most Asians excel in math and science?" "Are all or most Jews interested in making money?" "Are all or most African Americans learning disabled?" What are your prejudices? How do you know? What do you do to ensure that they don't affect your decisions as an educational leader? (Allport, 1987)

• Take action to combat bias. The explanation of impartiality in this chapter goes beyond simply assuming a neutral stance. Taking _action_ to combat oppression is an important responsibility of an educational leader. What action have you recently taken to demonstrate your impartiality? Check off which of the following statements describes you.

_____ I tell or listen to jokes that aim to put people down.

_____ I believe that most people in schools are not oppressed in any way.

_____ I am aware that oppression exists but I don't know what to do about it.

_____ I read books or attend workshops and seminars to learn more about these issues.

_____ I actively support others who speak out or take action against oppression.

_____ I consciously work to change individual and institutional actions and policies that discriminate against others. I also plan educational programs to combat bias and hate.

• Confront curricular bias. Although textbooks have improved in terms of ensuring nonracist and nonsexist presentation, problems persist. Form a committee of students, teachers, and parents to examine instructional materials to identify forms of curricular bias. Then (always taking an action) develop ways to remove these biases (Sadker & Sadker, 1999). Consider these seven forms of bias that may exist in various instructional materials and the samples given:

1. Invisibility: Do the materials omit African Americans, Latinos, and Asian Americans?

2. Stereotyping: Do the materials portray only Dynamically Aggressive men?

3. Imbalance and Selectivity: Do the materials make reference only to European discoveries regarding math and science?

4. Unreality: Do the materials gloss over unpleasant facts and events in history, such as whether or not Native Americans were the victims of genocide?

5. Fragmentation and Isolation: Do the materials present information in a fragmented way, such as providing an isolated box separate from the main textual materials entitled, "Ten Black Achievers in Science"?

6. Linguistic Bias: Do the materials describe non-English speakers as "alien"?

7. Cosmetic Bias: Do the materials suggest that they are bias-free by displaying a cover that is multicultural, when in fact the text narrative is exclusionary?

• Promote multicultural education. Examine your school or district through a multicultural lens. Multicultural education consists of five dimensions: (1) content integration, (2) equitable pedagogy, (3) empowerment of school culture and structure, (4) prejudice reduction, and (5) knowledge construction (Banks, 1997).

Why is impartiality such a vital virtue? Without maintaining an impartial stance, we conduct our affairs based on unexamined assumptions. All human behavior is fundamentally subjective and selective. However, an educational leader who intentionally considers options and alternative ways of thinking and behaving, and who promotes equity for all people, affirms and facilitates an educational environment conducive to learning and achievement for all.

Impartiality, then, is defined as the commitment to maintain a nonpartisan position on issues and to take an active stand against hate, bias, and all injustices.

How can we ensure that prospective and current educational leaders are impartial? We can begin by valuing impartiality and examining our beliefs and attitudes, particularly by considering how our beliefs and attitudes have influenced our thinking and actions. Unfortunately, there is no quick and easy survey to administer, and anyone can hedge on surveys, such as the one in Appendix B. You can ask and look for instances in which a person has demonstrated fair decision making and a commitment to bias-free education. Such an approach moves us toward understanding whether someone is impartial. Then, identify individuals who recognize oppressive practices in schools or districts, who educate themselves and others about oppression, who support and encourage antidiscriminatory practices, and who prevent individual and institutional actions that oppress others.

*Tolerance and fairness are the most important antecedents to equality of participation for all members of a society to analyze, argue, and resolve common issues.*

—CARL GLICKMAN AND RONALD L. MELLS
(Glanz & Neville, 1997, p. 347)

# 11

## Empathy

Aliyah Shehedah always wanted to be a principal. She felt that as a principal she could help many people. "I don't aspire to a position higher in the chain of command than principal. I want very much to help people while at the same time staying in touch with them on a daily basis." Shehedah's caring and sensitivity for others started as a child. Her mother recalls the warmth and compassion that Shehedah felt for the downtrodden and disenfranchised. "Aliyah always had the ability to sense another's suffering and pain. She could almost get inside their head and heart. She connects with all people."

During her interview for the principalship, she explained that teachers and parents are responsible for training children not to mock retarded or overweight children, or children who are unathletic, shy, or otherwise socially awkward. "One of the greatest cruelties occurs," explained Shehedah, "when children mock a peer because she or he comes from a poor family. I recall an incident that occurred when I was a teacher in another school in another district. A 13-year-old girl named Wendy attended this school largely made up of children from affluent families. She was often subjected to a barrage of disparaging remarks, ranging from the boy who insisted that she give up her bus seat ('Move over, trailer girl'), to the girl who responded to Wendy's question about where she had bought her beautiful new shirt by laughing and saying, 'Why would you want to know?' Wendy later explained that the reason she asked about the shirt was 'just to make small talk.' On another occasion, a classmate teased Wendy about her clothing and her humble home in the trailer park. He wouldn't stop, and finally, provoked, she kicked him in the shins. When he complained to the school authorities, they didn't punish him for his taunting words, but instead placed Wendy on suspension." Shehedah continued, "If parents, teachers, and administrators can't teach their children to empathize with another child's suffering, then all the other academic and social things we do for them are for naught."

Shehedah didn't just talk about empathy—she personified the trait. Teachers marveled at her ability to empathize with their experiences in the classroom. "She understands the problems I face. Unlike other supervisors, who once they leave the classroom forget what it's like to be a teacher, Ms. Shehedah cares and supports our efforts." Another teacher commented, "Ms. Shehedah is able to put herself in the shoes of the teachers. She realizes that only one disruptive student can cause havoc. She instituted a time-out policy to relieve us from some of the problems we have in the classroom." Another teacher summed up Shehedah's attitude best: "Ms. Shehedah is the most caring principal I have ever had the privilege to work for. She's not a pushover. She has high expectations for students and teachers. Yet, she is able to convey a sense of caring sensitivity, appreciation, and respect for the dignity of all people. She puts people first."

### Focus Questions

1. What would you guess are the indicators that Shehedah demonstrated empathy?

_____

_____

2. What factors may have contributed to her empathetic nature?

_____

_____

_____

3. How have you recently exhibited empathy?

_____

_____

4. Why is empathy so vital a virtue for an educational leader?

_____

_____

5. What are some other ways educational leaders can exemplify empathy?

_____

_____

What does it mean to be an empathetic leader? The word "empathy" conjures up images of individuals, usually female, consoling others in times of crisis or listening carefully to their suffering. What do caring, compassion, and empathy have to do with educational leadership? Why does a leader have to personify empathy to be considered a good leader?

The image of an administrator has been culturally ingrained as a bureaucrat and autocrat. Although not all administrators act that way, autocracy in school administration and supervision has been reinforced by the establishment and maintenance of bureaucratic school governance. Expectations are established for administrators to, first and foremost, maintain organizational stability and adhere to bureaucratic mandates. Authority to carry out their mandates is conferred through hierarchical status. In short, the organization, not the individual, is of paramount importance to such a school administrator.

Framing school leadership on a radically different paradigm— "leadership as ethic of caring" (Noddings, 1984, 1992)—is a more useful and potentially empowering concept of school administration.

Such a model strengthens the notion that our task as principals, for example, is essentially to support and encourage teachers while nurturing children by teaching them to be caring, moral, and productive members of society. As Noddings (1992) explains, "The traditional organization of schooling is intellectually and morally inadequate for contemporary society" (p. 173). By nurturing an "ethic of caring," principals, as well as teachers, realize that their ultimate motive is to inspire a sense of caring, sensitivity, appreciation, and respect for the human dignity of all people despite the travails pervading the world. Noddings (1992) writes, "We should educate all our children not only for competence but also for caring. Our aim should be to encourage the growth of competent, caring, loving, and lovable people" (p. xiv).

Feminist organizational theory (Regan, 1990) informs this "ethic of caring" by avoiding traditional concepts of leadership. Feminist theory questions legitimacy of the hierarchical, patriarchal, bureaucratic school organization. Challenging traditional leadership models, feminist theory sees community building, interpersonal relationships, nurturing, and collaboration as the primary interest. Regan's research suggests that women as educational leaders are more attuned to fostering intimate relationships that accentuate an ethic of caring. It seems reasonable, however, to think that both genders are just as likely to demonstrate that they are concerned with teaching, learning, instruction, curriculum, and people. Marshall argues that because women "spend more time as teachers and as mothers before they become administrators, they produce more positive interactions with community and staff; they have a more democratic, inclusive, and conflict-reducing style; and they are less concerned with bureaucracy" (Marshall, 1995, p. 488). This theory implies that the difference may not lie inherently in gender. Certainly there are women who can exhibit officious, domineering behaviors and demonstrate autocratic and bureaucratic tendencies. Conversely, there are some men who can be as nurturing and caring as women. Although women in our society and culture are more easily accepted as sensitive, sympathetic administrators and men less so, many men have the same capacity for caring and nurturing that are crucial in engendering a spirit and ethic of caring.

Unlike traditional humanistic models of administration, "caring" is inclusionary, nonmanipulative, and empowering. Whereas the main objective of bureaucracy is standardization, caring inspires individual responsibility. Starratt (1993) provides support for an ethic of caring in educational administration: An administrator committed to an ethic of caring is "grounded in the belief that the integrity of human relationships should be held sacred and that the school as an organization should hold the good of human beings within it as sacred" (p. 195).

How do educational leaders demonstrate caring and empathy? (1) They listen to all perspectives; (2) they respond appropriately to the awareness that comes from this reception, and (3) they remain committed to others and to the relationship. Moreover, caring and empathetic educational leaders

> frequently develop relationships that are the grounds for motivating, cajoling, and inspiring others to excellence. Generally thoughtful and sensitive, they see nuances in people's efforts at good performance and acknowledge them; they recognize the diverse and individual qualities in people and devise individual standards of expectation, incentives, and rewards. (Marshall, 1995, p. 282)

An empathetic leader, therefore, should put people first and policy second. All the leadership quality types have the capacity to demonstrate compassion, caring, and empathy at the high end of their quality continuum. Empathy is integral to the effectiveness of a leader.

## A Personal Lesson in Empathy

My father was a Holocaust survivor, and he denounced hatred of all kinds. Clearly, he had his reasons. Once, when I was in grade school, he and I were traveling on the Staten Island Ferry in New York City. A Hispanic family was seated across from us. They were poorly dressed and were having difficulty with English, a situation all too familiar to me, since my father was an immigrant from Poland.

Several young, rowdy hoodlums started mocking them. My father glared furiously at these ruffians. I saw the look and the response it elicited: the obnoxious boys were cowed and walked away, trying to save face by muttering, "Dirty Jew bastards."

My father later told me never to hate others for how they spoke or looked, and only to judge people by their actions, no matter who they were or what they looked like—an invaluable lesson I carry with me to this day. He could empathize with the Hispanic family and how the hatred affected them, and was able to use his empathy to avert a situation that might have escalated into more than nasty words and looks.

## Actualizing a Leadership Role

As an educational leader, you can best actualize your role as an empathetic leader if you

• Demonstrate through your actions that people come first. One time when I was a teacher, our car pool was stuck in a massive traffic jam on one of the major city thoroughfares. We eventually arrived, 45 minutes late. Although the principal had already heard why we'd been delayed, he shouted, "How dare you be so unprofessional!" When I tried to explain, he retorted, "You should have had alternate means of transportation." This principal had clearly not empathized with us. In his view, we should have anticipated the traffic and left home one hour earlier as he had done. Although this incident was one of life's minor travails, his treatment of us that morning, right or wrong, was upsetting. How have you recently demonstrated that people come first?

• Communicate caring. Improve your listening skills. The next time a staff member experiences a personal challenge, ask her what happened. Listen to the person, say you're sorry, and offer to help. That's it; that's all you can do (Noddings, 1992).

Why is empathy such a vital virtue? If you have empathy, you have compassion for others. If you demonstrate caring, that communicates to others that they are important, worthwhile, and esteemed individuals. Treating people with compassion encourages them to respond in kind, to you and to others. Such behavior inspires them to do their utmost to help others. What more can an educational leader hope for?

Empathy, then, is defined as the extent to which an educational leader can sense, identify with, and understand what another person is feeling. How can we ensure that prospective and current educational leaders are empathetic? We need to talk about and read literature that emphasizes an "ethic of caring." We need to value the individual above all else. This does not mean that we avoid punishment when appropriate. Punishing students for misbehavior, for instance, may indeed demonstrate an ethic of caring. Another example is principals who take the time to evaluate untenured teachers, thus demonstrating their concern that we hire and retain only competent teachers for our children.

> *Do what you can to show you care about other people,*
> *and you will make our world a better place.*
>
> —ROSALYNN CARTER
> FORMER FIRST LADY OF THE UNITED STATES

# 12
## Judgment

Brian Teng never thought that his duties as a vice principal would lead primarily to supervising halls and yards. Although he devotes as much time as possible to curriculum development and instructional supervision, working in an inner city school places inordinate demands on his noninstructional duties. Committed and empathetic to the needs of the students, Teng dutifully arrives at school each morning before almost anyone else, other than the custodian and security officer. Classes begin at 8:40 a.m., and the breakfast program begins at 8:00 a.m., at which time the school is officially open. Some parents send their children to school well before the start of the breakfast program, often as early as 7:10 a.m., to wait outside to be admitted.

Exasperated that some parents could be so insensitive as to force their children to wait outside the school even in the harshest days of winter, Teng faced a dilemma. Should he allow these students official entry into the building prior to 8:00 a.m.? "Making judgments is hard," explains Teng, "because invariably you make at least one person mad at you." Still, Teng thought that if judgments were based on fact, such as that the Board of Education regulations state that school starts officially at 8:00 a.m., most people would understand.

One child in particular refused to comply with the regulation and continually pleaded for early entry into the building. On one particular morning, when the temperature was below freezing, Teng allowed her inside the building to stand with the security guard. Later in the school year, that child's parent burst into the school building, shouting at the top of her lungs, "Why does my child have to stand here?! It's freezing!

Is she being punished?" Teng explained that the child really couldn't be allowed entry before the official start of the day for safety reasons and because it might set a precedent for other children and parents. To Teng's astonishment, the parent then threatened to have Teng "beat up if you don't let her all the way into the building." "Now, what was I to do?" queried Teng. Clearly, the child was at school too early, even though the parent was at home at the time. Also, the safety issue was a real concern. Neither the security guard nor he could constantly watch the girl as she sat or stood inside the building. "This was certainly a tough dilemma," Teng thought to himself. He could, of course, ask the principal for advice, but Teng decided that this would be good experience in learning how to assess a situation and make a decision based on a reasoned judgment. Teng thought to himself that he never learned about this kind of situation in graduate school

In spite of the parent's protestations and threats, Teng refused to allow the child early entry into the school building again until he could secure someone—a parent volunteer, perhaps—to watch the children before the breakfast program began. Teng realized that it wasn't the child's fault and that it was difficult to reason with some parents. He also knew that this parent's threat wasn't serious. "She just wanted to intimidate me. I thought I stuck to my guns. I make decisions by always thinking of what would be in the best interests of the children."

## Focus Questions

1. What are the indicators that Teng demonstrated good judgment?

---

---

2. What would you have done in a similar situation?

---

---

---

3. What factors should be considered when rendering a decision or making a judgment?

_____

_____

4. Why is judgment so vital a virtue for an educational leader?

_____

_____

5. What does it mean to possess good judgment?

_____

_____

The word "judgment" conjures up images of someone in authority rendering decisions in the manner of King Solomon (see the "The Wisdom of Solomon," p. 114). A good judge is said to possess much knowledge. Yet merely accumulating knowledge is not sufficient to be truly wise. Wisdom is the ability to take that accumulated knowledge and use it to think intelligently about a particular situation. Judgment is the ability needed to apply that knowledge sensibly.

In previous chapters we discussed the importance for leaders to possess courage, impartiality, and empathy. Clearly, using good judgment in making decisions is also important to an educational leader. Leaders may indeed act courageously (stand behind their principles), demonstrate impartiality (maintain a nonpartisan position), and exhibit empathy (identify with another's pain). Yet, without good judgment, educational leaders are completely ineffective because their good intentions may be misplaced or, worse, detrimental to the school or district. How does an educational leader learn good judgment?

Judgment is a special talent that cannot be taught, but it is gained through experience and practice. Possessing sound judgment means that one can make decisions intelligently. Judgment is the ability to consider the weight of various facts and information to determine their relevance to a particular situation. Hence, the ability to critically think is integral to good judgment.

Educational leaders are action researchers; they are detectives of sorts. They test the validity of various proposals by developing hypotheses and using them in the real world. Leaders collect an array of data to make decisions intelligently and are not neutral technicians who merely dictate policies without appropriate follow-ups. They possess professional knowledge and technical skills that enable them to analyze and solve problems with insight and imagination.

A leader who possesses good judgment, therefore, has the ability to sift through myriad data, select what's relevant, weigh it against the pressing needs of the moment, and make a valid decision. A leader who lacks judgment may possess other virtues, but is destined to fail because the crux of good leadership is the ability to make thoughtful, reasoned decisions.

### The Wisdom of Solomon

One of the most famous stories from the Bible's Old Testament (1 Kings 3:16–28) is about King Solomon, who reigned in Israel for 40 years during the 10th century BCE. According to the story, two women came before the king with two babies, one dead and the other living. Each woman claimed the living child as her own, and said that the dead child belonged to the other. The young king listened carefully to both women's explanations and asked for a sword to be brought to him. When the sword was brought in, Solomon said, "Take this sword, and cut the living child in two, and give half of it to each one."

One of the women cried out, and said, "O my lord, do not kill my child! Let the other woman have it, but let the child live!" But the other woman said, "No, cut the child in two, and divide it between us!"

Solomon then said, "Give the living child to the woman who would not have it slain, for she is its mother."

Solomon's decision, which at first seemed cruel, was in fact the brilliant strategy of a leader who possessed intelligence, knowledge, understanding, intuition, and good sense.

### A Case of Poor Judgment

As I was sitting in my office one day, a parent charged in and demanded to see me. As an assistant principal, my day was hectic and arduous. A parent complained that one of the teachers had struck her child. Despite the fact that I had a report due to the principal at 3:00 p.m. and had to complete an attendance report for the District Office by the next day, this parent needed my immediate focus. I stopped writing and gave her my full attention. But this good judgment on my part was short-lived.

About 10 minutes later, when I had just calmed down the parent, I received a call from the special education teacher that one of the male students was "hanging out of a window on the 4th floor." "So, what's new?" I said to myself, knowing the boy had often pulled this stunt to get attention. I told the teacher that I would be up as soon as I could. Not knowing what the call was about, the parent continued her tirade against the teacher who had allegedly struck her child, going so far as to say, "Wait till I get my hands on her!" Our conversation continued another 10 minutes, during which I succeeded in allaying her apprehensions, and she agreed to let me investigate the matter and report to her the next day.

Relieved at avoiding a parent-teacher confrontation, I headed for the 4th floor. By the time I arrived, however, the principal was already there, chastising the miscreant. I dispersed the crowd that had formed. After dealing with the child, the principal asked me to follow him to his office. In private, the principal berated me for not immediately "dropping what I was doing" to deal with a potentially life-threatening situation. Even though he admitted that the boy had exhibited this behavior several times, he explained that I needed to learn good judgment. "You must discern the difference between what is important [the parent and her complaint] and what is urgent [the student hanging out of the window]."

As I am writing this incident, I realize how ridiculous it may sound to you. Of course I should have first dealt with the student! But in the midst of the incident, it wasn't so clear or so easy. Keep this story in mind as you answer the following questions.

1. Have you ever experienced a bout of "poor judgment"? Explain.

_____

_____

2. What did my principal mean by differentiating what was important from what was urgent? Provide an example or two.

_____

_____

## Actualizing a Leadership Role

As an educational leader you can best actualize your role as a good judge if you

 • Sharpen your critical thinking skills. Anyone who has worked as a leader realizes that "educational leadership is riddled (or blessed) with situations that demand quick action and almost immediate response" (Beck, 1994, p. 128). Donald Schon (1987) describes a type of critical (reflective) thinking called reflection-in-action—the ability to "think on one's feet" when faced with the many surprises and challenges in our daily lives as educational leaders. Successful leaders are certainly able to think quickly as they face the multitude of crises that are all too common in school or district. Since judgment entails taking knowledge and applying it intelligently and, in most cases, "on the spot," no easy formula exists to ensure the best judgment. Practice is the best teacher, but developing critical thinking skills can't hurt. Consult many of the fine works that help sharpen your thinking skills; many of them are fun at any age (e.g., Paul, 1993).

• Engage in reflective practice. Schon (1987) also discusses a second type of reflective thinking, reflection-*on*-action. Reflection-on-action occurs when educational leaders look back upon their work and consider thoughtfully what practices were successful and what areas needed improvement. Too busy? Can't find the time? Try this suggestion and you'll discover that judgment making can be enhanced: Schedule time on your calendar, during the least hectic time of day (e.g., 1:45–2:00 p.m.) to close your door, take the phone off the hook, and consider one area that requires a careful decision (e.g., "Should I hire that new teacher candidate?").

• Undertake action research. Action research is a powerful tool of disciplined inquiry that enables a leader to carefully and systematically reflect on practice. Follow these four easy steps: (1) select a focus of concern; (2) collect data; (3) analyze and interpret the data; and (4) take action (Glanz, 1998).

The possession of knowledge does not guarantee that you can succeed in educational leadership, or that you will exercise good judgment with respect to work in a particular area. Good judgment in the context of educational leadership requires that the leader have a firm grounding in the educational enterprise (e.g., be well versed in all areas of education), combined with a keen sense of awareness of the complex factors that impinge on school practice.

Good judgment requires knowledge, reflection-in-action and reflection-on-action, and the ability to consider a wide array of factors, sometimes simultaneously and immediately. How can we ensure that prospective and current educational leaders are capable of good judgment? Intelligent decision-making skills can be developed by giving leaders a solid background in educational leadership and offering them situations to resolve in simulated situations. These simulations, however, even when combined with readings that might inspire good judgment (e.g., "The Wisdom of Solomon") are insufficient. Judgment is a special gift that cannot be taught, but it can be learned through experience. Identifying prospective leaders who possess good judgment is as difficult, perhaps more so, as finding leaders with other virtues. Leaders who appear thoughtful, are consensus builders, and who realize the importance of action research are likely to possess good judgment.

> *Judgment, a critical element in*
> *leadership decision making, has two components.*
> *One is knowledge. A leader cannot make a judgment*
> *if he is unfamiliar with the subject about which the*
> *judgment must be made. . . . The other component*
> *is common sense, which is an attribute that*
> *individuals attain through experience.*

—GENERAL ROBERT H. BARROW

# 13

## Enthusiasm

Carol Krute never thought she would ever assume the superintendency of any district, let alone her own. In her positions as teacher, staff developer, principal, and curriculum director, Krute was always known as a diligent, dauntless, thoughtful, fair-minded, caring educator. Still, no woman had ever reached the superintendency in her district. Although she thought she had the requisite skills for the job, she set her sights on just doing the best job she could for students and teachers.

Krute possessed many fine qualities, but one stood out above all the rest. "I have never seen anyone as enthusiastic and devoted to her job as Carol," wrote a former superintendent about Krute's work in the district as curriculum director. "Her enthusiasm is intoxicating and contagious," reflected another colleague. "Although she is ardent, resolute, and committed she is not overly so, not fanatical. Rather, she is deliberate in her actions and genuine in her feelings. She inspires us all."

Krute got her wish. A school board member who knew Krute's reputation recruited her as the superintendent. "We've had some good leaders as superintendents here," said the chair of the board. "These leaders were well organized and knowledgeable. They were, however, boring bureaucrats who didn't inspire anyone to do anything beyond their specific responsibilities." She continued, "We need someone who can turn our schools around by rallying everyone around excellence. Ms. Krute has what it takes." Krute, elated at this new opportunity, took the bull by the horns and got to work. Within a few years, she turned around a dead-end district with little more than a bundle of enthusiasm. Although she worked in one of the poorest-performing districts in the city, Krute raised standardized test scores and overall performance significantly.

Praise for her efforts came from several school board members, who commented on her assets during an annual review:

- She loves her job and it shows.
- Everyone who interacts with Ms. Krute senses her genuine interest and concern.
- She confronts every activity with so much fervor that it's contagious.
- Carol is constantly on the move—endless parent and community meetings, phone calls to politicians, one-on-one meetings with teachers, principals, and parents—she goes on and on.
- Ms. Krute possesses many skills but her enthusiasm for what she does sets her above all the rest. She leads by example. She's the most energized person I've ever met.
- Her enthusiasm is monitored. She's not a cheerleader. She is attuned to the problems teachers and principals face daily. Yet her optimism and will to succeed are remarkable qualities to which I attribute to the improved performance of the schools in our district.

### Focus Questions

1. How can enthusiasm for one's job "turn around" a classroom, school, or district?

_____

_____

2. What factors may have contributed to Krute's enthusiasm?

_____

_____

_____

3. Why is enthusiasm so vital a virtue for an educational leader?

_____

_____

4. What does it mean to be an enthusiastic leader? The word "enthusiastic" conjures images of motivational speakers and pep rallies. Do educational leaders have to serve as cheerleaders? Can enthusiasm really make a difference? Why does a leader have to personify enthusiasm to be considered a good leader?

_____

_____

_____

In my research, I have surveyed thousands of educators across the nation and around the world. One of the questions I posed was, "What is the number one quality of a good leader?" Overwhelmingly, respondents identified "enthusiasm for one's work" as most important. Ironically, students often complain that their teachers are boring. Can you remember sitting in a class where the teacher was not enthusiastic about his work? Can you recall what a difference an enthusiastic teacher made? What about the same for leaders you've known?

Enthusiasm demonstrates passion for your work. Passionate people enjoy what they do and are often successful. Moreover, such enthusiasm is inspiring. Consider some of the world's great leaders. They possess enthusiasm and optimism. They inspire others to action.

Enthusiasm is not a skill. It is not something that you can develop after taking a course. Rather, it is a state of mind. Enthusiam combined with optimism is the awareness that the glass is half full, not half empty. Optimism is a way of looking at the world with the belief that one can indeed make a difference. It is a virtue that all successful leaders possess. Consider the following quotes from famous leaders.

*No dream is too big for those with their eyes in the sky.*
—Buzz Aldrin, astronaut

*Excellence! The attitude generates enthusiasm, attracts top people, and becomes the basis for real optimism.*
—Robert Schuller, religious leader

*A leader is a dealer in hope.*
—Napoleon Bonaparte

An enthusiastic leader views the world and difficult situations, not through rose-colored glasses, but with an abiding sense of the positive; that possibilities exist where others see hopelessness. Enthusiasm is not generated merely in situations of crises, but is evident as leaders go about their daily work. Displaying genuine interest in your work is key to successful educational leadership.

Some leaders inspire others through their deeds, still others through their words. Enthusiasm resounds in their choice and delivery of words. Consider, for example, "I Have a Dream," by Reverend Dr. Martin Luther King Jr. (Bruun & Getzen, 1996).

1. Have you ever heard a leader give a speech that motivated you to action or energized you?

_____

_____

2. What is it in "I Have a Dream" that demonstrates enthusiasm, idealism?

_____

_____

_____

3. Do you think that reading speeches of various leaders can enthuse you?

_____

_____

## Actualizing a Leadership Role

You can best actualize your role as an enthusiastic leader if you

• Fine-tune your values. If you have a firm set of beliefs and values, you are most likely to exhibit enthusiasm while trying to actualize them. What are your educational beliefs and values? What do you want for students? teachers? schools? Make a list of your beliefs about teaching and learning, about teachers, about supervision, about instructional leadership, and about yourself. How do these views influence your commitment to actualizing them?

• Increase levels of enthusiasm. Although a self-help approach has been avoided in this book, enthusiasm has a lot to do with quality levels. The healthier a person is, the more likely he is to be able to sustain long periods of work. An effective educational leader requires the physical and mental stamina to endure many arduous challenges. Diet and physical exercise are critical. Avoiding coffee and junk foods, for example, is a good start. Commonplace in schools, these foods actually drain your energy. What seems to be an initial high soon leads to drowsiness, disinterest, and apathy. Instead, eat something nutritious—grains, seeds, or a natural granola bar. The long-range effects of negative eating habits weigh on your physical and mental well-being. Exercise (e.g., a brisk walk three times a week) boosts quality levels.

Leaders cannot be trained in enthusiasm; it's a natural characteristic. Although nearly anyone can feign enthusiasm for a short time, it's tough to pull off the act over time. We can, however, enhance our enthusiasm by identifying and adhering to a belief system. Why? A genuine desire to impart what we believe to be true and important is a significant impetus for enthusiasm. Enthusiasm is the state of being in which one exudes fervor about something that is of value or importance.

How can we ensure that prospective and current educational leaders are enthusiastic about education? Discover what motivates them: What are they interested in? What do they value? What do they want to accomplish? Listen to their responses. Do they excite you?

> *I studied the lives of great men and famous women, and I found that the men and women who got to the top were those who did the jobs they had in hand, with everything they had of quality and enthusiasm and hard work.*

> —HARRY S. TRUMAN

# 14

## Humility

Osborne Donmoyer had reason to be proud. The first in his family to graduate college, Donmoyer also earned two master's degrees and an Ed.D. in educational administration from Teachers College at Columbia University. His mother was proud of her firstborn child. Watching her son ascend the podium to receive his degree, Mrs. Donmoyer glowed with excitement and pride. Donmoyer's good fortune continued in the ensuing months as he secured a principalship in one of the finest schools in New York City.

Donmoyer had what it took to be a fine principal. Prepared and confident, he addressed the faculty during the first faculty meeting outlining his bold vision for the school. "I can't do it alone. I need your help as much as you need mine. And the same goes for the parents. They need us but we need them too. Reaching out to all stakeholders, including custodial and secretarial staff, is essential if we are to become true partners in this educational enterprise." Donmoyer continued to articulate his academic and instructional goals and objectives while stressing the importance of collaboration and shared vision. Nearing his conclusion, he reminded teachers how important "our job really is. . . . We are charged with awesome responsibilities, and the rewards, although not always immediate and obvious, are nonetheless profound and significant." Extolling the virtues of education and the role that educational leaders (teachers and principals) play, Donmoyer told his audience that "as we recognize our duties and obligations to the children and parents who are our clients, we must fully appreciate the magnitude of the trust placed in us by the citizens of this nation. That recognition impels us to acknowledge our limitations and strive to reach out to anyone and everyone who can assist in this important challenge we call education." Underscoring his personal humility as principal and the reverence he has for teachers and the process of education, he then related an experience that changed his life.

"I wasn't always aware of the importance of humility. Allow me, if you will, to share an experience that changed my attitude forever. I was the first person in my family to go to college. At the time, I was full of my accomplishments and myself. It was 1968 and I was immediately drafted. I was not a happy camper, but choices were slim for a patriot. So, off to war I went, even if it was begrudgingly.

"I was in boot camp and found myself 'company commander.' After all, I was a college graduate and I was intelligent and confident. My charge was to move a group of 40 other men through 8 weeks of the unknown. I tried everything I could think of, but I was not finding success in getting 'my team' together.

"It was not until four weeks into the training that I had my epiphany. It came at the hands of one Master Chief Bob Tate, a man small in stature, but huge in wisdom. I approached the encounter with bravado you would not believe. After all, I was a college graduate and he was nothing more than an enlisted man. It was a terrible mistake that I had not gotten into Officer Candidate School and had to suffer with this group of 'low lifes.' I was surely going to let this guy know just how I felt about his Navy.

"Needless to say, the meeting did not go as I had planned, but, in hindsight, it surely went the way Chief Tate had planned. I was laid open from top to bottom, with a little physical involvement thrown in for good measure. After 60 minutes of the greatest comeuppance a guy could have, Chief Tate's closing comment to me was, 'you may have graduated from college, but you've been to a fool's school until you've been to the school of life. You've got the potential to be a good leader, but until you get your head out of your ass, there's no one on this God's given earth that will follow you anywhere.' Tate was a poor African American, who did not go past the 6th grade in school; he had distinguished himself in two wars—Korea and Vietnam. I have carried this lesson in humility with me since. More than once, it has helped me move through difficult times."

**Focus Questions**

1. What would you guess are the indicators that Donmoyer demonstrated humility?

_____

_____

2. Why is humility so vital a virtue for an educational leader?

_____

_____

3. What are some other ways educational leaders can exemplify humility?

_____

_____

4. What does it mean to be a humble leader? The word "humility" conjures up images of subservience, deference, and meekness, qualities that seem antithetical to a leader. In fact, leaders are invested with authority within the educational hierarchy. They have high salaries, a separate union, their own offices, and even reserved parking spaces. Moreover, leaders are usually highly credentialed and have special advanced certifications. They are usually more experienced than teachers, who are lower in the hierarchy. How and why should leaders exhibit humility?

_____

_____

Many peoples' understanding of humility is skewed. Many think that demonstrating humility indicates low self-esteem. The truth is that the more confident a leader is, the greater capacity she has for humility. Humble leaders prefer to stay in the background not because they are shy, reticent, or insecure. They are confident and secure enough in their own accomplishments to herald the achievements of others. As one leader put it: "I prefer to act in such a way that my assets are not trumpeted on my sleeve, but rather are known by my actions." Humble leaders are not "proud of their humility." The challenge for good leaders is to learn how to negotiate the delicate balance between expertise and humility.

Pretentiousness, arrogance, and conceit are anathema to good leaders. Good educational leaders do not hold on to dogmatic beliefs about "best practices" in the face of poor results. No one has a panacea to solve all the schools' problems. In contrast, the prototypical autocrat lacks humility and is devoid of respect for children and their teachers.

A humble leader, therefore, acknowledges the tentativeness of his suggestions and also respects teaching and teachers.

## William Hare on Humility

Hare (1993) has a great deal to say about this "taken-for-granted" virtue. Here are some of his thoughts on the subject.

> None of this [acknowledging the tentativeness of one's position] is a general argument for diffidence and hesitancy in the classroom. It could be equally misleading to suggest to students that we have grounds for being uncertain, other than the general ground of human fallibility, when we do not. (p. 37)
>
> Two lessons about humility might be taught in this way: one, that it is not assumed that all the answers are in; two, that it is not suggested that the teacher's own answers are obviously the best. (p. 36)
>
> It [humility] serves rather to offset the kind of self-satisfaction which interferes with a recognition of the possibility of,

and need for, *improvement*. The absence of humility . . . would impede progress. (p. 40)

A good teacher recognizes that there is much that he or she does not know, but it is a fallacy to think that one will be a better teacher if one knows less. (p. 42)

## Actualizing a Leadership Role

You can best actualize your role as a humble leader if you

• Empower others and give them the credit. As a confident leader, you can empower others in school improvement initiatives. You lead by example and are ready, willing, and able to stand in the background to allow others to take the credit. As long as you are attaining your objectives, you are not concerned about receiving all the credit. A good leader is one who can empower others to exhibit their own leadership qualities to achieve a greater good. Robert Woodruff, founder of Coca-Cola, said, "[A leader] can accomplish great success if he doesn't care who gets the credit" (Blumenthal, 2001).

• Highlight the accomplishments of others. Identify deserving individuals and find ways to positively reinforce and acknowledge Herculean efforts on behalf of the school or district. Acknowledge them continuously, not just in an end-of-year letter. Humble, secure leaders reward others for a job well done. Leaders who do not acknowledge others often don't do so for a variety of reasons, including personal insecurities ("If I acknowledge John, then they'll think he ran the show"), frustrations ("Well, no one ever acknowledges my accomplishments"), and the belief that people don't deserve rewards ("After all, that's why he's getting paid"). Humble leaders realize the importance of highlighting the accomplishments of others.

Humility is indeed a virtue often ignored and may, as Stephen Covey (1990) intimates, be the prerequisite for all other virtues. Humble leaders, though, live paradoxically. On the one hand, they realize their strengths, accomplishments, and capabilities; on the other hand, they are cognizant of limitations. These leaders lack arrogance, affirm the abilities of others, and eschew personal accolades. These self-effacing leaders are highly respected and beloved in the organization, though you rarely find humility discussed in literature on leadership. Having humility is being aware of your limitations while being cognizant of your abilities.

How can we ensure that prospective and current educational leaders are humble? Listen to how they talk about themselves and others. Do they only recite their accomplishments and what they alone can do for the organization? Do they respect and acknowledge the contributions of others? Do they value collaboration? Are they aware of their ignorance about certain matters? Are they confident enough in their abilities to empower others to participate in school or district reform efforts? Do they strut their humility? Or do they appear to be gentle yet secure? Do they reflect your image of true humility?

*I know nothing except the fact of my own ignorance.*

—SOCRATES
(As found in Hare, 1993, p. 43)

# 15

## Imagination

Edith O'Hare always viewed the world differently from most people. Optimistic and visionary, O'Hare believed in the possibilities of individuals to accomplish great things, even when the odds were not in their favor. As a student teacher, her creativity was evident to all. She was a risk taker. She rarely, if ever, used the teacher's guide, and tried innovative ideas in teaching her lessons. Even while being observed in class, she was willing to try new ideas. As a teacher and vice principal, she was known for her creative qualities: O'Hare involved parents by starting a "take a picture with your child" campaign (inviting parents to be photographed with their child on picture day) and a telephone and e-mail hotline for parents to receive information daily about their child.

The school board selected O'Hare as principal because they needed someone who would break the school out of stagnation, do things differently, set new parameters for achievements, and, as one parent put it, "reach for the sky."

Before her appointment, many teachers, parents, administrators, and even students held low opinions of the school. O'Hare, by simply redefining the need of the school within the community, was able to reshape opinion. Using imaginative ways to create a community of learners—inviting parents to volunteer when it was convenient for them, engaging community agencies (e.g., churches, local businesses, social agencies) as partners, restructuring traditional grade-level activity—this principal defined a new way of doing old business. O'Hare took the abstract and made it real for students—she showed them the rewards of hard work and connected what was taught in the classroom to their lives. On the whole, O'Hare was able to demonstrate for all stakeholders new ways of doing things by breaking through the walls of pessimism that had been built up after years of neglect, mismanagement, and unimaginative leadership.

O'Hare encouraged others, especially teachers, to try new ways of doing things. Not against traditional methods if they worked, she advocated and conducted workshops on innovative instructional practices such as Web-based instruction, cooperative learning, and alternative assessment. She instituted an intervisitation program that encouraged teachers to observe their colleagues, and gave them release time to make it happen. O'Hare was the first principal in the district to adopt the voluntary alternative supervision model based on cognitive coaching. She gave teachers release time to partake in action research projects and involved faculty and students in discussions about adopting a block schedule format in schools.

O'Hare was always open to new possibilities, new ways of improving the schools. "I don't believe that every innovation that comes along is worth attention. However, I'm not close minded; I'm open to new ideas. I think it is crucial for all educational leaders to, in Maxine Greene's words, 'pierce the webs of obscurity. . . to break through a world taken-for-granted . . . to see and then to choose.'"

**Focus Questions**

1. What would you guess are the indicators that O'Hare demonstrated imagination?

_____

_____

2. What factors contributed to her use of imagination?

_____

_____

3. What is the relationship between imagination and creativity?

_____

_____

4. Why is imagination so vital a virtue for an educational leader?

_____

_____

5. What are some other ways educational leaders can exemplify creativity and imagination?

_____

_____

6. What does it mean to be an imaginative leader? The word "imagine" conjures up "dreamy" images of some high-flung, pie-in-the-sky ideas divorced from the reality of school practitioners. What does imagination mean to the educational leader? What does it mean to behave imaginatively as a leader? Why does a leader have to personify imagination to be considered a good leader?

_____

_____

Discussions of leadership, especially in the context of educational administration, infrequently focus on imagination. Attention is generally focused on less esoteric, more practical considerations such as instructional strategies and organizational frameworks. It is regrettable that much work in educational leadership is uninspiring, mechanical, and unimaginative. Only by focusing on imaginative leadership can reform and school improvement efforts take on new meaning and can progress be made. Progress requires creative thought. Creativity is what you do with your imagination. Creativity may take many forms. Leaders may create new schedules, develop unique lessons, and brainstorm solutions to problems.

Leaders who possess initiative, independent thinking, and imagination are very much needed. Imaginative leaders formulate alternative solutions, consider alternate interpretations, seek other possible explanations, think of new questions, and design meaningful experiments.

Provincial thinking, therefore, is not the hallmark of imaginative leaders. They are too inventive, innovative, and forward-looking for that trap.

## Just Imagine

Imagine what you would do in each of the following situations. Obviously, there is no right answer. Compare your ideas with those of a friend, perhaps a Creative Assertive, especially if you are not that quality type.

- You're a vice principal in a high school—a girl wants to join the senior football team. What would you do?

_____

_____

_____

- You're a staff developer—your overheads were left on your desk at home. You have to present in five minutes to a group of fellow staff developers. What would you do?

_____

_____

_____

• You're a teacher—You've been asked to present a workshop on creative ways of teaching math to students at risk for fellow teachers in your school. What would you do?

_____

_____

• You're a guidance counselor—your caseload of students has been doubled because of budget cuts. What would you do?

_____

_____

• You're a school librarian—you've been asked to develop a Web-based instructional unit on J. F. Kennedy for 11th grade social studies classes. What would you do?

_____

_____

• You're a dean of students—you've been informed that you must implement Canter's Assertive Discipline program in your school this fall; you've never heard of this program. What would you do?

_____

_____

• You're a principal—the superintendent asked you to represent the district at a state conference on alternative assessment. What are some issues you might raise?

_____

_____

• You're a director of curriculum—newly hired in a district known for its failing grades in math. Teachers complain that they've been "workshopped out." What would you do?

_____

_____

_____

• You're an assistant superintendent—the superintendent asks you to evaluate the district's gifted program. How would you do it?

_____

_____

_____

• You're a superintendent—the school board has hired you to bring new life to the district's stagnant arts program. What would you do?

_____

_____

_____

_____

• You're a professor of education—your chair asked you to develop an alternative to faculty supervision in the department. What would you do?

_____

_____

_____

_____

• You're a dean at a university—you have an accreditation visit in one year and your faculty has not revised the course outlines. What would you do?

_____

_____

_____

## Actualizing a Leadership Role

You can best actualize your role as an imaginative leader if you

• Create a think tank. Ideas are what drive an organization toward improvement. Generate ideas by establishing a think tank in your school or district. Identify key individuals who possess great imagination. Gather them together for weekly or biweekly meetings. Identify specific areas of concern and brainstorm solutions. Bring the ideas generated to other faculty or staff for group consideration. Refine and crystallize the ideas. Develop a hypothesis or a set of research questions for field testing. Monitor progress but always value the development of ideas.

• Create a democratic learning community. Imaginative leaders move the organization from established practice toward emerging practice. Imagine new ways of viewing learning: Learning is no longer conceived as predictable but rather as a complex and differentiated process. Teaching moves from simply rote methods to informed reflective judgments. Supervision is no longer concerned with ensuring adherence to bureaucratic regulations; it is focused on helping teachers discover and construct professional knowledge and skills. Teachers and supervisors are no longer isolated and independent technicians, but collegial team members, mentors, and peer coaches. Schools are no longer bureaucratic teaching organizations; they are democratic teaching and learning communities (Sergiovanni, 1996).

Imaginative leaders investigate new ways of doing things. They develop new ideas in situations that seem hopeless. Imaginative and creative leaders encourage others to examine their taken-for-granted ways of doing things. They upset the proverbial apple cart by being free thinkers. Imagination is the power to see what others can't.

How can we ensure that prospective and current educational leaders are imaginative? Listen to how they talk about ordinary ideas and concepts like school, education, learning, and teaching. Do they toe the line or do they come up with fresh ideas? Do they seek to maintain the status quo or do they want to try new ideas? Are they willing to risk some failure? Do they attend conferences to generate new ways of doing things? Are they lifelong learners? Are they dreamers?

*Imagination is more important than knowledge.*

—ALBERT EINSTEIN

# 16

## *Importance of Leadership Virtues*

Chapters 9 through 15 introduce seven leadership areas of excellence, or virtues, that different people can manifest (see Figure 16.1). Leaders can exhibit any or all of these virtues in varying degrees. However, each leadership virtue is essential for good leadership. We must move from superficial criteria or competencies when selecting our leaders and emphasize the fundamental areas of human virtues. A critical understanding of what a good leader is results in identifying leaders with "desirable intellectual, moral, and personal qualities" (Hare, p. 161). Regrettably, educators have shied away from these qualitative assessments and often rely on presumed identifiable and measurable competencies or skills.

A good leader has unique predispositions. If you took the survey in Appendix B, you can identify the degree to which you possess these virtues. If you were honest in your responses, you have an idea which virtues you clearly possess and which you lack. An initial reaction to taking the surveys might be to say, "Well, I may not be very courageous, but I am nonetheless imaginative and I do make good judgments." Remember that these virtues should be viewed as a fluid continuum between extremes (see Figure 16.2, p. 141). You may not possess the extreme imaginative talents of a Creative Assertive, but you may be able to tap into your creative reservoir to some degree in given situations. You may not possess the courage of a Dynamic Aggressive, but you can manifest sufficient courage on occasions. Although I argue that these virtues are essential for any leader, I realize that few, if any, people can personify them to their utmost all the time. The point is to use these surveys as a means for self-reflection and, ultimately, improvement.

Although most of us possess one particular leadership quality, we can learn lessons and modes of behavior from other quality types to some degree while maintaining our natural inclinations. Similarly, although you may possess several virtues to lesser degrees, you can indeed learn to strengthen and personify certain virtues. All leadership quality types must exhibit, or at least try to exhibit, these virtues to effectively lead.

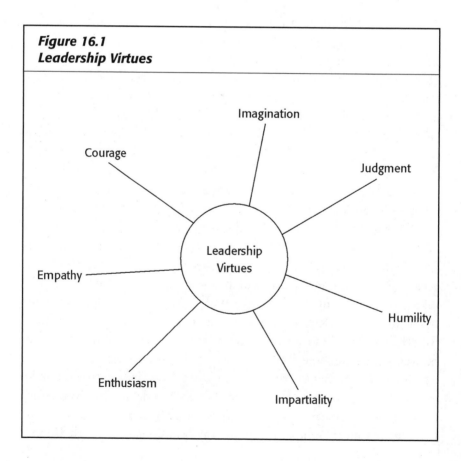

**Figure 16.1**
**Leadership Virtues**

Clearly, different qualities and virtues may be necessary for specific circumstances or situations. For example, if I were forming a committee to offer recommendations for statewide educational reform, I would make certain that several Creative Assertives, Dynamic Assertives, and people who personify great imagination were included on the committee. A committee composed only of Adaptive Assertives and Adaptive Supportives might not yield the necessary radical changes.

---

**Figure 16.2**
**Leadership Virtues Continuum**

←————————————|————————————→

| Low end | High end |
|---------|----------|
| Cowardly | Courageous |
| Biased | Impartial |
| Indifferent | Empathetic |
| Poor judgment | Good judgment |
| Dull | Enthusiastic |
| Arrogant | Humble |
| Unimaginative | Imaginative |

*Note:* Do not view this continuum only at its extremes. Individuals may exhibit these virtues in varying degrees.

---

Schools cannot renew themselves by choosing leaders who are cowardly, biased, indifferent, poor at judgment, unenthusiastic, arrogant, and unimaginative. They need leaders who are aware of their own ignorance, but who are not afraid to stand behind programs and practices that are controversial; leaders who are committed to treating people (children, parents, and others) fairly and justly, while engendering enormous passion about their work; leaders who can appreciate and sense others' hurt and who can weigh complex factors in rendering decisions; and finally, leaders who are capable of stepping outside the boundaries established and entrenched by the bureaucracy.

Educators must rethink their goals and refocus their emphases on the enduring and profound qualities we want our leaders to possess. Beyond technical competence, do we want leaders with a limited sense of their moral, intellectual, and personal qualities? Or should we demand leaders who are ethical, empowered, and confident? Do we want leaders who are arrogant, dogmatic, and insensitive? Or do we want leaders who have humility, courage, and empathy? The answer to these questions depends largely on the kinds of leaders we want in schools or districts. Given the increasing complexity of problems and issues facing schools, do we really have a choice?

Which virtues do you manifest? What unique leadership contributions can you make to the school organization? Are you a good educational leader? How do you know?

# PART THREE

# Enhancing Leadership Qualities and Virtues in Yourself and Others

*Leadership takes many forms.*

—THOMAS SERGIOVANNI

# 17

## Actualizing Natural Leadership Qualities

You now understand your Natural Leadership Quality (N.L.Q.). How you developed this tendency is not as important as learning how you can refine or enhance your proclivities, how you can work toward the high end of the quality continuum, and how you can expand your potential by learning from other quality types (see Figure 17.1). Equally vital is identifying qualities in others and matching their unique contributions with the demands and requirements of the school organization.

This chapter translates N.L.Q. theory into concise, practical information for school leaders by offering (1) surveys for each quality group to assess where you operate on the continuum; (2) suggestions for enhancing your personal and professional leadership qualities; (3) ways you can learn from other quality groups; and (4) ideas for recognizing leadership qualities in others and capitalizing on these talents for the benefit of the school or district.

## N.L.Q. Continuum: High End and Low End

Although you were introduced to the leadership qualities, you now need to assess how you function at your best. As a reflective practitioner, you are interested in self-improvement and seek to serve as an effective school or district leader. To help you function at the higher end of your quality continuum, identify your quality type in the following pages, take the appropriate survey, and answer the follow-up questions. For these surveys to assist you, honest responses are required. Although you should take the survey in private, I recommend sharing and discussing your answers with someone who knows you. Do not feel that you *must* share the results, however, and remember that no one functions at the highest end of the leadership quality continuum all the time.

---

**Figure 17.1**
**Learning from Each Leadership Quality**

| | |
|---|---|
| Dynamic Aggressives (DAG) | Affinity for hard work |
| Dynamic Assertives (DAS) | Sociability |
| Dynamic Supportives (DS) | Sense of humor |
| Adaptive Aggressives (AAG) | Problem solving and optimism |
| Adaptive Assertives (AAS) | Good organization |
| Adaptive Supportives (AS) | Unflappability |
| Creative Assertive (CAS) | Independent thinking |

---

## Dynamic Aggressive Continuum

Read each pair of sentences and check the one that describes you. In some cases, check both sentences if you already have a particular trait or quality, but would like to develop it further.

1. _____ I am achievement-oriented.
   _____ I'd like greater drive and motivation.
2. _____ I enjoy the company of many.
   _____ I enjoy time alone.
3. _____ I tell it like it is.
   _____ I would like to speak up at times.
4. _____ I am aggressive in pursuing a goal.
   _____ I could be more aggressive.
5. _____ I'm responsible and hard working.
   _____ I procrastinate.

6. _____ I'm tolerant and fair with others.
   _____ I want to develop my integrity.
7. _____ I'm a good leader.
   _____ I could be a better leader.
8. _____ I trust my fellow workers.
   _____ I distrust people; they must earn my loyalty.
9. _____ I am terrified of intimacy.
   _____ I want to develop deeper personal relationships.
10. _____ I know I have charisma.
    _____ I'd like to develop more charisma.
11. _____ I crave attention.
    _____ I prefer being alone.
12. _____ I know who I am.
    _____ I'd like to learn more about myself.
13. _____ Money, power, and prestige are important.
    _____ Money, power, and prestige are not important.
14. _____ I am trustworthy and ethical.
    _____ I wish I were more trustworthy and ethical.
15. _____ I love my children unconditionally.
    _____ My children must earn my love.

Examine your responses. How do you know for certain that your answers are honest? Share your responses with someone close to you and ask them if they agree with your assessment of yourself. In addition, if you are a Dynamic Aggressive, what areas would you like to improve?

_____

_____

_____

_____

_____

_____

## Dynamic Assertive Continuum

Read each pair of sentences and check the one that describes you. In some cases, check both sentences if you already have a particular trait or quality, but would like to develop it further.

1. _____ I have courage to combat injustice.
   _____ I wish I had more audacity.
2. _____ I'm a good follower.
   _____ I need to be a better follower.
3. _____ I'm a good problem solver.
   _____ I want to be a better problem solver.
4. _____ I'm honest and trustworthy.
   _____ I could be more honest.
5. _____ I am satisfied with myself.
   _____ I am depressed.
6. _____ I don't mind change.
   _____ I manipulate others easily.
7. _____ I am people-oriented.
   _____ I am conceited.
8. _____ I am cooperative with others.
   _____ I am competitive.
9. _____ I like to think.
   _____ I think too much.
10. _____ I care for others.
    _____ I can be rude and uncaring.

Examine your responses. How do you know for certain that your answers are honest? Share your responses with someone close to you and ask them if they agree with your assessment of yourself. In addition, if you are a Dynamic Assertive, what areas would you like to improve?

_____

_____

_____

_____

_____

_____

_____

## Dynamic Supportive Continuum

Read each pair of sentences and check the one that describes you. In some cases, check both sentences if you already have a particular trait or quality, but would like to develop it further.

1. _____ I'm physically and emotionally healthy.
   _____ I wish I were more so.
2. _____ I'm friendly.
   _____ I need to be more selective.
3. _____ I have healthy, positive relationships.
   _____ I'd like to have better relationships.
4. _____ I have empathy for (understanding of) others.
   _____ I'm too empathetic.
5. _____ I'm kind and I care for others.
   _____ I need to care more about myself.
6. _____ I balance things in my life and job well.
   _____ I tend to procrastinate.
7. _____ I deal well with change.
   _____ I could handle change better.

Examine your responses. How do you know for certain that your answers are honest? Share your responses with someone close to you and ask them if they agree with your assessment of yourself. In addition, if you are a Dynamic Supportive, what areas of would you like to improve?

_____

_____

_____

_____

_____

_____

## Adaptive Aggressive Continuum

Read each pair of sentences and check the one that describes you. In some cases, check both sentences if you already have a particular trait or quality, but would like to develop it further.

1. _____ I'm honest and trustworthy.
   _____ I need to be more honest.
2. _____ I have a good imagination.
   _____ I'd like to improve this ability.
3. _____ I know when to be loyal and obedient.
   _____ I'd like to be more loyal.
4. _____ I'm a good problem solver.
   _____ I want to be a better problem solver.
5. _____ I'm self-assured.
   _____ I'm not as self-assured as I may appear.
6. _____ I can take criticism.
   _____ I should learn to accept criticism.
7. _____ I'm emotionally stable.
   _____ I'm emotionally volatile at times.
8. _____ I have many true friends.
   _____ I wish I had more friends.
9. _____ I'm personable.
   _____ I want to develop deeper personal relationships.
10. _____ I know I have some charisma.
    _____ I'd like to develop more charisma.
11. _____ I crave excitement.
    _____ I need to learn how to relax.

12. \_\_\_\_\_ I strive for self-improvement.
    \_\_\_\_\_ I better spend more time on self-improvement.

Examine your responses. How do you know for certain that your answers are honest? Share your responses with someone close to you and ask them if they agree with your assessment of yourself. In addition, if you are an Adaptive Aggressive, what areas would you like to improve?

_____

_____

_____

_____

_____

_____

## Adaptive Assertive Continuum

Read each pair of sentences and check the one that describes you. In some cases, check both sentences if you already have a particular trait or quality, but would like to develop it further.

1. \_\_\_\_\_ I act responsibly.
   \_\_\_\_\_ I am overly cautious.
2. \_\_\_\_\_ I conserve things and I'm thrifty.
   \_\_\_\_\_ I am neurotic about these matters.
3. \_\_\_\_\_ I'm able to forgive others and myself.
   \_\_\_\_\_ I want to learn how to forgive more easily.
4 \_\_\_\_\_ I'm tolerant and fair with others.
   \_\_\_\_\_ I need to be more tolerant.
5. \_\_\_\_\_ I'm very organized and neat.
   \_\_\_\_\_ I'm ridiculously compulsive.

6. _____ I have direction and purpose in my life.
   _____ I'd like to have more direction or purpose in my life.
7. _____ I'm self-disciplined.
   _____ I could be more self-disciplined.
8. _____ I'm predictable.
   _____ I'm unimaginative.
9. _____ I'm happy with my life.
   _____ I feel no need to change anything.
10. _____ I seek intellectual and spiritual growth.
    _____ I wish I was more emotional.

Examine your responses. How do you know for certain that your answers are honest? Share your responses with someone close to you and ask them if they agree with your assessment of yourself. In addition, if you are an Adaptive Assertive, what areas would you like to improve?

_____

_____

_____

_____

_____

_____

## Adaptive Supportive Continuum

Read each pair of sentences and check the one that describes you. In some cases, check both sentences if you already have a particular trait or quality, but would like to develop it further.

1. _____ I take care of myself physically.
   _____ I should take better care of myself.
2. _____ I'm a calm and peaceful person.
   _____ I need to be more calm and peaceful.

3. _____ I'm a good follower.
   _____ I need to assert myself more.
4. _____ I can lead if I want to.
   _____ I prefer to be alone.
5. _____ I'm responsible and hard working.
   _____ I make poor decisions.
6. _____ I have integrity. I walk the talk.
   _____ I want to develop my integrity.
7. _____ I am courageous.
   _____ I wish I would take a stand.
8. _____ I trust my fellow workers.
   _____ I distrust people; they must earn my loyalty.
9. _____ I am loyal to my principal.
   _____ I am too trusting of those in authority.
10. _____ I fear the unknown.
    _____ I am not afraid of change.
11. _____ I'm stubborn.
    _____ I wish I was less inflexible.

Examine your responses. How do you know for certain that your answers are honest? Share your responses with someone close to you and ask them if they agree with your assessment of yourself. In addition, if you are an Adaptive Supportive, what areas would you like to improve?

_____

_____

_____

_____

_____

_____

_____

## Creative Assertive Continuum

Read each pair of sentences and check the one that describes you. In some cases, check both sentences if you already have a particular trait or quality, but would like to develop it further.

1. _____ At times, I can work endlessly.
   _____ I get tired after a short time of work.
2. _____ I enjoy creating something new.
   _____ People say I'm creative, but I don't think so.
3. _____ I'm happy most of the time.
   _____ I wish I could be happy at will.
4. _____ I'm an independent thinker and doer.
   _____ I rely too much on authority figures.
5. _____ I'm a thinker more than a doer.
   _____ I wish I accomplished more than I do.
6. _____ I'm frequently optimistic.
   _____ I wish I were more optimistic.
7. _____ I'm a good leader.
   _____ I could be a better leader.
8. _____ I handle stress well.
   _____ I need stress management sessions.
9. _____ I want to succeed.
   _____ I have a fear of failure.
10. _____ I am driven to create.
    _____ I need encouragement in order to create.

Examine your responses. How do you know for certain that your answers are honest? Share your responses with someone close to you and ask them if they agree with your assessment of yourself. In addition, if you are a Creative Assertive, what areas would you like to improve?

_____

_____

_____

_____

_____

_____

_____

## Know Who You Are

You can't change if you don't know who you are. Knowing yourself requires self-assessment and, perhaps even more important, feedback from others. Confirm your personal assessments with the opinions of those whom you trust.

**Strategy 1.** Gather at least five different viewpoints by asking five different people you trust to describe you. Do their descriptions confirm or contradict your assessment of yourself?

**Strategy 2.** In the self-help section of your local library, select and read a book that deals with uncovering people's strengths and weaknesses.

**Strategy 3.** Spend a day in conscious self-reflection. Conduct your normal business, but observe carefully how you interact, for instance, with others in the workplace. Are you overbearing? Are you congenial? How do you know that they appreciate your point of view? What do you think they might say behind your back?

### Affirm Your Values

What do you believe in? What do you want to accomplish? How do you view teachers, students, and administrators? Articulate your core beliefs and values about education. Align your values with practice.

**Strategy 1.** Develop a mission statement for yourself. Refer to it and act on it—every day.

**Strategy 2.** Share your mission statement with trusted colleagues and ask them for feedback about the extent to which the statement matches your actions as a leader.

**Strategy 3.** Every six months, review your goals and objectives as articulated in the mission statement and revise as necessary.

## Know That You Want to Change

Some people are not compelled to change. For instance, I know an Adaptive Assertive who realizes his compulsiveness and inflexibility, but is content. If you, on the contrary, want to improve yourself, start small—identify two specific areas that you want to work on. For example, Jose Guerrero is a Dynamic Aggressive who has been told and has accepted the fact that he is rather domineering and arrogant. He'd rather not act that way, especially when he works with his teachers. He wants to change. The first step on the way to change is awareness.

**Strategy 1.** Set up a suggestion box for suggestions, comments, and ideas. The data may surprise you. Some data may help you become aware of things you might not know, and suggestions may be directed at you. Think about the data and assess how useful change may be.

**Strategy 2.** Ask yourself periodically, "If I changed (a certain behavior), how might my job performance improve?" This strategy works well with individuals who are aware of their strengths and limitations. Someone who is compulsive, for instance, might attempt to be less so when he sees that compulsivity can lead to poor job performance.

**Strategy 3.** Identify several individuals you work with and think about what they might change to increase their performance. Are they likely to change? Do they want to change? How might they be encouraged to change? Sometimes thinking about others can encourage personal growth and change.

## Use the KISS Principle

Keep It Simple, Silly. The key word is simple. Start slowly by selecting one specific aspect you want to change. Maude Bok is aware that she is domineering and self-centered. What can she do? She decides to monitor her talk during committee meetings. She decides in advance of the meeting not to say a word during the first 20 minutes, to limit her comments after that, and to solicit others to share their views. Although later in the meeting she may assert her view, she will do so thoughtfully without forcing her opinions on others.

**Strategy 1.** Take an index card and write down the KISS principle. Post the card on your bulletin board or keep it on your desk. Refer to it occasionally and ask yourself, "How might I best employ this principle today?"

**Strategy 2.** Share the KISS principle with others and suggest ways they might develop solutions that are uncomplicated. One of the best ways to learn something is to teach it.

**Strategy 3.** Identify other areas for improvement and start to work on them one by one, realizing that the process is sometimes more important than the product.

## Learn from Other Qualities

You enhance your own quality by learning from and about others. Ask yourself, "What can I learn from Bill, who is an Adaptive Supportive?" Realize the importance of team effort. Build leadership teams with members from various quality types. Often, teams or committees are formed out of expedience or volunteerism. Bring people together who have special talents and qualities to contribute to specific tasks.

**Strategy 1.** Observe others. Identify two or three individuals in the school or district you respect and perhaps even want to emulate. What qualities do they possess that are particularly noteworthy? How might you learn to manifest these qualities or characteristics?

**Strategy 2.** In private, role-play how it might feel to act dynamically, for instance. If you are not a Creative Assertive, you may role-play an instance in which someone important has asked you to join a team and generate ideas for improving the school or district. What might you suggest or offer as possibilities?

**Strategy 3.** Use the KISS principle to identify one area for improvement. Work on it until you can incorporate it in your repertoire of skills.

## Practice Responsible Leadership

Effective leaders build integrity and character through their work. To paraphrase Peter Drucker (1999), good leaders lead not through the knowledge and skills they possess, but through responsibility and integrity (p. 2). Use your unique quality to offer responsible leadership. Leaders lead responsibly when they are true to their leadership quality. Irresponsible leaders are unaware of how they affect an organization. These leaders abuse their positions by working for themselves rather than for the benefit of all constituents.

**Strategy 1.** Read biographies or autobiographies of great leaders.

**Strategy 2.** Ask yourself, "What effect do I have on the school or district organization?" "How might the organization function differently if I were no longer around?"

**Strategy 3.** Become an avid reader of books and articles on leadership. Although some books are repetitive, learn to appreciate the fact that even one lesson learned is an invaluable opportunity for personal growth and improvement.

## Serve—You Are a Leader

Leadership is not invested in the select few. How can you contribute to improving the school or district? Don't relegate leadership to others by abrogating your responsibility. Find out how you can assist, and do so willingly and consistently.

**Strategy 1.** Do not let a day go by without asking someone if she needs assistance.

**Strategy 2.** Volunteer when others are reluctant.

**Strategy 3.** Ask, "How might I bolster the image of my school or district by serving in some capacity in the outside community?"

## Never Compromise on Quality

You enhance your quality by striving for excellence. Commit to quality, and accept nothing less from yourself or from others. To attain this goal, read the books recommended as a strategy. As you read, identify leadership characteristics you feel can enhance your personal commitment to excellence.

**Strategy 1.** Mark F. Goldberg's *Lessons from Exceptional School Leaders*.

**Strategy 2.** Linda Lambert's *Building Leadership Capacity in Schools*.

**Strategy 3.** Joyce Kaser, Susan Mundry, Katherine Stiles, and Susan Loucks-Horsley's *Leading Every Day: 124 Actions for Effective Leadership.*

## Honor Your Quality

Flaws and all, each person has worth and needs to actively participate in school or district renewal.

**Strategy 1.** Ask, "What are my strengths?" "What are my weaknesses?" "How can I best serve the school or district?" "What do I need to do or change to have a more sustained impact?"

**Strategy 2.** Identify leadership qualities in others. Encourage someone who doesn't realize his potential for leadership. Serve as a personal mentor in an informal way and discuss with him how he might serve as a leader in the school or district. Call on him to take a more active role.

**Strategy 3.** Don't compromise the integrity of who you are. Don't be made to feel that you have to function more dynamically, assertively, or creatively. Know who you are and appreciate the unique contributions you can make to the school or district.

## Enhance Your Virtue

Enhance your leadership quality by seeking to accentuate the universal leadership virtues (see Chapter 18).

**Strategy 1.** Retake Survey 3, Assessing Your Leadership Virtues (p. 199), in Appendix B and affirm the virtues that you manifest most and least. How might these results help you to better strive for excellence as a leader?

**Strategy 2.** Identify those virtues that need improvement. Using an index card for each virtue, describe what you might do to enhance the virtue in the workplace and even in your personal life. Keep the card handy and refer to it occasionally.

**Strategy 3.** Don't forget that leaders personify each virtue to the best of their ability. The goal should be to strive to achieve maximum excellence in each virtue. Ask yourself, for each of the virtues, "What do I need to do to [become more courageous]?"

## Things You Can Learn from Others

Regardless of our leadership quality and inclinations, we can all grow, learn from others, and incorporate alternative ways of thinking and behaving to enhance our effectiveness as leaders. Figure 17.1 (p. 146) summarizes one idea we can learn from each of the seven qualities.

### Dynamic Aggressives

They have a natural affinity for hard work. Since they are goal-oriented, Dynamic Aggressives have a plan and an agenda to accomplish and achieve. Although other quality types also work diligently, Dynamic Aggressives really enjoy the effort they expend. They are risk takers and aggressively pursue their objective. Identify someone who possesses this quality—watch her and then try to emulate her to some degree.

### Dynamic Assertives

They are people-oriented and appreciate how much they can learn from associations with many people. Although Dynamic Assertives may have some lifelong friends, their relationships with others grow and change all the time. These relationships change over time because Dynamic Assertives need to learn from and experience others. If you are not as naturally sociable as this quality type, intellectually you know that it is important for school leaders to socialize. Watch a Dynamic Assertive and go out of your way (just once a day) to spend five minutes talking with him about business and making small talk.

### Dynamic Supportives

Of all the quality types, Dynamic Supportives have the best sense of humor. They know how to enjoy themselves and appreciate the humor in most circumstances. Their easygoing, optimistic demeanor contributes to the aura of affability. If people tell you that you're too serious, try listening to audiocassettes on humor and joke telling. It may not make you into the life of the party, but the strategy helped me.

## Adaptive Aggressives

They are excellent problem solvers. Adaptive Aggressives see a problem or a crisis as an opportunity and a challenge. They do not give up a battle easily; they work the system to accomplish their goals and understand the importance of politics in any situation. Understand that politics, for better or worse, is part of your job as leader. Seek out politically resourceful individuals and consult them often.

## Adaptive Assertives

They are neat freaks and prefer to work in an ordered environment. Adaptive Assertives keep their desks at work and home extremely ordered. They have good time management skills. Does this description sound different from you? Observe Adaptive Assertives and start small, by organizing just one file. Realize that your style of organized chaos might work well at times, but that it can sometimes get you into trouble. As a last resort, hire an Adaptive Assertive assistant.

## Adaptive Supportives

At the high end, they work hard but know how to relax and leave their work at the office. Find it hard to relax? I know it's hard for some quality types (see Creative Assertives) to understand the laidback style of Adaptive Supportives. Still, observe their easygoing style. Talk to them. Get to know them and see how and when you can turn off the motor.

## Creative Assertives

They are independent thinkers, the doers and creators. They do not need the limelight. In fact, they prefer long periods of time in isolation from others. Isolation is time spent either in contemplation of an upcoming project or in actual creation. Are you always on the go? Watch someone from this group. Schedule meditative time. No interruptions (barring real emergencies). Plan activities, such as deep breathing exercises, and use the time to think about a special project.

Obviously, these are just samples of the lessons we can learn from each other. As reflective educators, we need to explore other ways of enhancing our leadership abilities. How might you enhance your leadership quality?

## A Stress Tip

Although learning from others is important, you will fall back on your most comfortable quality. The most fundamental way, then, to actualize your natural leadership quality is to know that you live and work in harmony when you accept and work at your quality level, especially at the high end. Each leader should be encouraged to express her quality as fully as possible. When our proclivities are not given expression (e.g., Dynamic Aggressive women who are coerced to act in Adaptive Supportive ways), disappointment, anger, suppression, and even disease can set in.

One of the major impediments to actualizing our potential is stress. Educators are exposed to stressful situations every day. Teachers confront recalcitrant students who irk them, public school administrators encounter irate parents who try to sabotage an upcoming board meeting, and professors receive rejection letters for manuscripts from peer-reviewed journals right before tenure. Stress is inevitable. How we deal with stress is critical to our well being. Each of us deals with stress differently depending on our natural life quality.

• Dynamic Aggressives. As a rule, Dynamic Aggressives are under the most stress of any quality group because of their demanding positions and lifestyle. Yet they do not tend to deal with stress well. They seldom analyze the causes of their stress, therefore they react viscerally and don't devote sufficient time to stress reduction strategies. Moreover, their fast-paced and hectic lifestyle does not allow serious attention to self-improvement strategies. Still, they persist, and their dynamic quality enables them to accomplish much.

• Dynamic Assertives. They are also under a lot of stress, but they tend to deal with it well. The assertive part of their nature compels them to discover strategies that help them to deal with stress effectively in various situations.

• Dynamic Supportives. When Dynamic Supportives are under

stress, they may not deal with it well because they are busy helping others with their problems. As a result of this selfless approach to others, they tend to neglect their personal welfare. Be aware of this tendency and seek assistance. Self-help tapes and books can be useful.

• Adaptive Aggressives. Adaptive Aggressives thrive on stressful situations. Their adaptive qualities enable them to deal effectively with stress while their aggressive qualities get the job done.

• Adaptive Assertives. Because of their compulsivity, Adaptive Assertives are often anxious and nervous people. They are easily stressed. If not taught coping strategies, they have difficulty dealing with life's crises.

• Adaptive Supportives. Adaptive Supportives are usually the least stressed quality group.

• Creative Assertives. By contrast, Creative Assertives do not deal well with stress because of their sensitivity and volatility.

The observations about stress and the leadership qualities are generalizations. Individuals vary in their reaction to stress. Still, keep in mind the general tendency of your type to put you in an optimal position to cope with stress. The point is that the degree to which you know who you really are determines how effectively you deal with life's stresses.

## Recognizing and Working with Leadership Qualities

Identifying and realizing your own leadership quality is important. Equally important is to learn to work well with other leaders. Leadership does not occur in a vacuum. Your effectiveness is measured to a large extent by your ability to recognize leadership talents in others and to collaborate with them for the improvement of the school or district.

### Dynamic Aggressives

They eagerly seek challenges and love the thrill of adventure and competition. They are highly goal-oriented. Consequently, Dynamic Aggressives do not waste time on what they consider inane pursuits. Activities that do not contribute to their goals are not considered worthwhile. This quality group is more concerned with important issues such as organizational policies and educational reforms. Dynamic Aggressives conceptualize large ideas and are often the boss. Here are some suggestions for working with them:

• Acknowledge their quality type. They are not like most people. Their dynamic qualities are essential and are used to inspire others and move the organization to higher levels of accomplishment.

• Understand their strengths. Are they innovative thinkers, achievement-oriented, and politically astute? Dynamic Aggressives can easily motivate others simply by their presence. Since they are often good orators, they influence and motivate others by their excellent presentations. They often use symbolic phrases, as did Martin Luther King Jr. ("I Have a Dream").

• Realize their limitations. Are they ruthless manipulators, self-serving bureaucrats, and inconsiderate of the feelings of others? Are they usually intolerant of others who have less ambition and drive than they do? Do they get easily frustrated and, at times, experience fits of anger and even depression? Do they struggle with humility? Accept them for who they are.

• Know what you can and cannot do. You may develop close relationships with Dynamic Aggressives, but they may not be willing or able to accept criticisms of their behavior. Understand where they are on the quality continuum. Dynamic Aggressives are intelligent; if they possess the positive virtues (i.e., humility, enthusiasm, empathy), they can improve their skills and relationships and become more effective leaders.

• Give them what they need. Give them the big picture when you advise them. Brief them on the sociopolitical situations that exist inside and outside the school setting. Talk about goals and the extent to which they are being met. Also, brief them on the details of a project. They may not be able or willing to actually work on details, but they want to know what is happening.

## Dynamic Assertives

They are not provincial thinkers. Like Dynamic Aggressives, Dynamic Assertives see the big picture, where others just see the details. They understand the impact of change on the entire organization. Moreover, they tend to understand the political realities of a situation within an organization. Dynamic Assertives understand the forces of power, authority, and vested interests. They work within this context to effect the changes necessary to achieve the larger goal. They are trailblazers, explorers, and risk takers. They do not fear the lone trail. People are attracted to their unique ideas. Dynamic Assertives are quite articulate and can easily convey their message using symbolic verbal imagery. When they speak, they do so from the heart and have the ability to communicate difficult ideas and concepts in ways that other people can readily understand. They are sensitive to other people's perspectives and experiences. And Dynamic Assertives have lots of ideas about how to improve things. Here are some suggestions for best interacting with them:

• Appreciate their accelerated pace. They are always tinkering and crafting new ways of doing things. Encourage their participation and insights. Offer them the tools they need to actualize their vision.

• Respect their need for privacy. Unlike Dynamic Aggressives, members of this quality group may prefer solitude for prolonged periods of time to energize their creative juices. Allow them the time they need to rejuvenate.

• Use their unconventional approach. They view situations and problems differently from the way you and I do. Appreciate their unique perspectives.

• Allow them to express themselves. Perhaps more than any other group, they tend to move rapidly toward the lower end of their quality continuum, especially when their views are not heard. Although their insights may not always be acceptable or feasible at present, provide them opportunities for expression.

• Understand their limitations. They have difficulty understanding why other people are so provincial and myopic. People who do not share their world view easily frustrate them, especially when they are unable to actualize the changes they advocate. Their frustration easily turns to anger and resentment. Understand this aspect of their personality and recognize their strengths.

## Dynamic Supportives

They are easily identified by their outgoing and friendly nature. Dynamic Supportives are driven to help others and have a hard time refusing anyone. They are more people-oriented than any other group. They are emotionally and spiritually sensitive. Dynamic Supportives are laid-back individuals. They are content with themselves and have nothing to prove to anyone. More than likely, they act sensitively and compassionately. Here are some suggestions for interacting with them:

• Accentuate the personal perspective. They are especially sensitive to people and the challenges they confront. They are good problem solvers when it comes to resolving interpersonal conflicts. In meetings, emphasize or delegate authority related to working with individuals or groups.

• Accept their rhythm. Since they are attuned to their emotional-spiritual self, they are particularly sensitive to the needs of other people. This natural quality forms the basis by which they understand and solve interpersonal problems. They are not usually amenable to structural or organizational means of solving issues.

• Encourage them to relax. This group does not handle stress well, especially on their down side, because they wear themselves out from helping others with their problems. As a result of this selfless approach, they tend to neglect their personal welfare. Encourage them to take a break, a day off, or even a vacation.

• Realize their limitations. People constantly request assistance from them. These requests may overwhelm them. When Dynamic Supportives are overwhelmed because they have not placed limits on their time, which happens because of their confident quality, they are prone to burnout and depression.

Dynamic Supportives have faith in people's capacities for improvement and good will and are disheartened to learn that someone has betrayed their trust. Also, since they sometimes neglect personal needs, you should be alert to this syndrome and ask yourself how you might assist them.

## Adaptive Aggressives

They are very cunning and socially astute. They are also extroverted, egoistic, and restless. They are goal-oriented and pursue their goals aggressively, no matter what the consequences. Adaptive Aggressives are good planners. They get bored easily unless they are actively involved in varied activities or projects, often preferring them to be simultaneous. Since they are wheelers and dealers, this group loves situations that allow them to roll up their sleeves and get to work. Socially and politically aware, they enjoy the thrill of conferencing and negotiating. Adaptive Aggressives have a strong drive to succeed. They are strategy-driven and seek power. More than likely, they make things happen in your school or district. Here are some suggestions for interacting with them:

• Get to the point. They are fast movers as they work to get things accomplished. They have little time and patience for chit-chat. When they request information, provide them with what they need as soon as possible. Similarly, in conversation, forego the pleasantries and get to the point to facilitate the relationship.

• Realize their shortcomings. Although all leadership qualities have shortcomings, Adaptive Aggressives are potentially dangerous people on their down side. They can be manipulative, tricky, and dishonest. Sometimes their words belie their actions. In such circumstances, be wary.

• Acknowledge their strengths. Nothing gets done without their participation. Assign members of this quality group to a project when you need to get it accomplished. Carefully monitoring their progress mitigates negative behaviors.

• Treat them with respect and kindness. Adaptive Aggressives have difficulty developing sincere, trusting relationships, especially when they have been emotionally hurt. Being burned may result in their tending to manipulate and mistreat people. You can counterbalance such behavior by going out of your way to act nicely, respectfully, and caringly (if you're a Dynamic Supportive, you won't have difficulty doing this). If they sense a genuine concern for them, this quality group has the potential to respond in kind.

## Adaptive Assertives

They make really fine supervisors and are most fulfilled in these roles. They are detail-oriented, support the status quo, and are conscientious—you can depend on them to take care of the details in organizing any program. They are orderly and predictable. Adaptive Assertives are not power hungry, nor do they crave attention. They need and want to fit in; it's the adaptive quality in their nature. Here are suggestions for interacting with them:

• Provide them with the overall objective and resources. Under most circumstances, they do not establish the vision for an activity or program. However, when given an overall framework and adequate resources, they can effectively put the idea into action. Step back at this point and allow them to work their magic.

• Give them positive reinforcement. Although all the quality types appreciate acknowledgement for efforts, Adaptive Assertives especially need this reinforcement to persist in their efforts.

• Remind them to relax. They are dependable, diligent workers who need little supervision. You can be certain that they are not slacking off during the job. They tend to work long and hard, but their overzealous behavior may cause them to experience considerable negative stress. Tell them they are doing a good job and that they are ahead of schedule. Encourage them to take a few hours off or even the day.

• Know what they can and cannot do. Although this is good advice for everyone, particular attention should be paid to the strengths and weaknesses of Adaptive Assertives. They are superb practical leaders, but they need to be surrounded by naturally creative individuals (see Chapter 7). Also, since they tend to display autocratic and bureaucratic behaviors on their down side, they benefit from the direction of a Dynamic Assertive whom they especially admire and respect.

## Adaptive Supportives

Although they do not appear to be natural leaders, they are invaluable in effectively running any organization or in accomplishing a specific leadership function, albeit narrow, within the organization.

Adaptive Supportives are loyal, respectful individuals. You can count on them to conform to established rules and regulations. Unlike Dynamic Assertives, Adaptive Supportives do not think of rocking the boat. They are not interested in supervising others or coordinating big projects or programs. They seek responsibilities for leadership, but on a small scale. Here are some suggestions for interacting with them:

• Remember that everyone can lead in some way, to some degree, at some time in a given situation. Adaptive Supportives are not natural leaders. They prefer to stay in the background. Yet, whether you are a Dynamic Aggressive or an Adaptive Assertive, you must realize that Adaptive Supportives have assets that can contribute enormously to an organization. Determine how best to use their talents. Identify an area of need on a small scale (e.g., working with a small team of students or even a few teachers on a grade level) and encourage and empower them to assume some responsibility. Support them by offering positive reinforcements. Don't forget that they are not motivated primarily by monetary enhancements (as might be an Adaptive Aggressive). Address their inclinations to offer assistance to people and stress how invaluable they are to the organization.

• Relate to their charitable, happy-go-lucky, and people-oriented nature. Adaptive Supportives are good-natured, caring individuals. On their high end, they are happy, functional workers. Support their need to be accepted by offering them frequent encouragement. If you need assistance with a project or an individual, encourage them to help by explaining the benefits their participation will have on the students.

• Understand that they are not likely to change easily. They are set in their belief systems and they fear change. They may listen to your suggestions regarding personal or professional change, but they are unlikely to substantially alter their behaviors and actions. If you remember that they, like horses, can be only led to water, you can avoid frustration when working with them.

• Accept their limitations. Since they prefer stability to change, they don't accept new things easily. Introduce curricular changes, for instance, gradually. Realize that their reluctance is not a statement against you or the new program; it's simply their natural disinclination to change. Work with them patiently; they will adapt (after all, they are "adaptives!").

## Creative Assertives

They are introspective and creative individuals. More than likely, they inspire you with their imaginative powers. Creative Assertives work at an intense pace—when they feel the need to create they can sit for hours, even for days.

Creative Assertives definitely march to a different drummer and look at the school organization differently from most people. Here are some suggestions for interacting with them:

• Realize that Creative Assertives view the world differently. They are not like most people. Their creative qualities influence their unconventional behavior and actions. Acknowledge their talents and involve them in projects that require outside-the-box thinking.

• Provide them with flexible schedules and minimize bureaucratic demands. To every extent possible, give them options and choices. For example, let them decide how best to complete a project. Making people with this quality type adhere to a fixed schedule or set routines stifles the creativity you want them to display and use.

• Realize their mood swings. They are emotionally charged individuals who may, on their down side, experience a lack of confidence, pessimism, and, more than most, stress. Establish working environments where their talents are readily and consistently rewarded. Allow Creative Assertives down time to deal with their mood swings. This may mean, for example, extending the time certain reports are due so as not to place an inordinate amount of pressure on them. Again, realize that people are different and require different approaches.

• Tolerate their eccentricity. They are naturally creative and have a hard time communicating with others less imaginative and tolerant of their views. Match them with Dynamic Assertives and other Creative Assertives.

## Leadership Qualities in Practice

The following case study illustrates how to recognize leadership talents in others and collaborate with them in a team environment.

Marsha Simpson is assistant superintendent for curriculum and instruction at Laurelton School District in El Dorado Hills, California. In light of recent supervisory cutbacks, Marsha's primary objective for this academic year is to identify leaders throughout the district to help promote instructional excellence; she plans on doing this by using Costa and Garmston's Cognitive Coaching model. A Dynamic Assertive, Marsha has the foresight to realize that she cannot do this alone. She realizes principals are often busy and cannot spend the quality time necessary to mentor or coach teachers. Most of the principal's time is spent on checklist observations and evaluations. In this urban district, assistant principals are burdened by overseeing yard and lunch duties and handling disciplinary matters. Consequently, Marsha knows she has to reach out for other instructional leaders.

Chris Jones has been teaching in the district for 15 years and is considered by his colleagues and supervisors as an outstanding teacher. Although reluctant to volunteer to assist the school or district beyond his classroom in the past, Chris has recently met with Marsha who convinced him to serve as a lead teacher to work with two beginning teachers at his school. Chris recently completed a master's degree program in supervision at a local college. He specialized in cognitive coaching. Chris believes that the task of a cognitive coach is to uncover possible hidden thought processes among teachers. Guided reflective activities enhance a teacher's perceptions and decisions, which produce positive teaching behaviors. Chris realizes that building and maintaining trust is one of the coach's primary goals.

Tatiana Whitaker is an 8th grade teacher in her second year at Elms Middle School who has a global, intuitive teaching style. Michelle Quinnoes is a 7th grade teacher whose style is detail-oriented and analytical. Both teachers volunteered for cognitive coaching and agreed to work with Chris Jones. Chris was given release time to work with them over a four-month period. Marsha was impressed with Chris's earnestness and success at establishing rapport with these two relatively inexperienced teachers. During the time that Chris was working with them, Marsha continued to identify other potential supervisory lead teachers in the district. She identified a team of eight teachers, most of whom did not have experience with cognitive coaching. Encouraging them to share their teaching expertise with others, Marsha conducted workshops for them on cognitive coaching. Marsha later approached Chris to also work with these teachers since he was so knowledgeable in cognitive coaching.

Marsha shared N.L.Q. theory with the team in order to help them understand that leadership is a shared responsibility and that leaders come in all shapes and sizes. The team that Marsha assembled varied in leadership qualities. Although Chris was the only Creative Assertive among the group, four Dynamic Supportives, two Adaptive Assertives, and two Adaptive Supportives assisted him. The team learned to build on each other's strengths. They shared pedagogical and supervisory approaches. They also discussed strategies based on their leadership qualities for working with beginning teachers who had different qualities. Over time, the team members were able to identify other potential supervisory leaders. Within a relatively short period, the program that Marsha established to enhance instructional improvement by capitalizing on diverse leadership qualities received state and national attention.

## Recognizing and Working with Leadership Qualities in Others

Recognizing leadership talents in others and working well with them is important. N.L.Q. theory also comes in handy when making hiring or job placement decisions. It is very important to match the job requirements with the right quality type. For instance, if the job entails prescribed, highly detailed work requiring good organizational skills, you wouldn't want to assign a Creative Assertive or a Dynamic Aggressive. Rather, an Adaptive Assertive or an Adaptive Aggressive would be the best choices. Many educators are mismatched with their assignments. Examine individuals who work in your school or district carefully. Armed with insights on leadership qualities, determine if each person is matched properly with job and role expectations. In cases where mismatches occur, you might try to counsel the individuals. Offer them assignments well suited to their quality level. Although you have little control over individuals in current roles, keep their qualities in mind when these individuals apply for other positions. For example, if you are looking for a strong, charismatic superintendent who has the political know-how to bring together "warring" factions in a district, seek a Dynamic Aggressive or Assertive and not an Adaptive Aggressive or Assertive.

Distributing the N.L.Q. survey to every person you meet is not feasible. Review the characteristics of each quality carefully and begin to observe behavior patterns among those you meet. Ask yourself: "What drives this person?" "How does he react in crises?" "How do others describe him?" These and other questions will assist you in recognizing the various quality groups. Once you are somewhat proficient in this skill, you must realize a fundamental premise of N.L.Q. theory—namely, building on people's strengths and matching their natural abilities and inclinations with the right role in the school or district. Don't try to change people. Each person is talented in a different way. Help others discover who they really are and allow them to participate in the school or district organization at their level of competence and interest. Schools and districts will flourish when N.L.Q. theory is understood and applied. The key to a successful school or district is in its people. N.L.Q. theory helps us understand their talents and how they can best serve.

# 18

## Tips for Enhancing Your Leadership Virtues

"**Y**ou mean I need to be courageous, impartial, empathetic, enthusiastic, humble, imaginative, and a good judge? Ugh . . ." The message of this book is that yes, effective leaders possess these qualities. Beyond using the definitions and explanations in this book, here are suggestions for enhancing the virtues within yourself and for identifying virtues in others.

### Courage

I've known for a long time that I'm not particularly courageous; the results from the survey in Appendix B affirmed this knowledge. My first inclination is to avoid conflict by taking the easy way out. I realize that this lack of will to stand up for certain issues can be a serious problem, or at least has the potential to be. Realizing this deficiency, I have taken steps to enhance this virtue. What I have done might be instructive for many readers.

First, I acknowledge my tendency not to take risks. Therefore, to counter this proclivity, I overcompensate. I purposely take bold steps to assert myself in certain situations. Second, I read accounts of courageous leaders and the steps they have taken. These accounts are inspirational and condition me, so to speak, to act similarly. Third, I take small steps. For example, I may take a risk when the stakes are not so high. Success breeds success. In fact, I have become so successful that some of my colleagues may be surprised to learn that I consider myself to lack courage.

**Impartiality**

Taking a nonpartisan position doesn't come naturally for most people. People often make prejudgments about others and events. If you have a difficult time maintaining a neutral stance, try these suggestions:

• When confronted with a situation that requires neutrality, be aware of your initial tendencies to pass quick judgment. Repeat to yourself, "I will remain neutral. I will weigh the evidence first."

• Take an active role in combating hate, discrimination, and genocide. Join a group that supports these worthwhile efforts.

• Check yourself often. When a situation presents itself that demands neutrality on your part, perk up, pause, and think, "I need to remain impartial."

**Empathy**

My guess is that you, as an educator, have little difficulty with this virtue. However, all of us can improve in some way. Does your empathetic nature compel you to action? You may hear about the plight of the Sudanese being enslaved, but are you impelled to action? If not, take action. You can best enhance this virtue by moving beyond the "feeling" stage and taking proactive and definitive steps that demonstrate your empathy. What steps have you taken? What steps can you take in the future?

**Judgment**

One of the critical questions raised when discussing these virtues (and qualities, for that matter) is, "Can someone really enhance a quality he may not really possess at all or very little?" On the one hand, I believe that qualities are, for the most part, natural conditions that are reinforced environmentally (i.e., through life's experiences). On the other hand, virtues can be developed to a far greater degree. That's why I maintain that, no matter what leadership quality you possess, you can exhibit all virtues (indeed, you must do so for effective leadership). However, not every leader is equally "virtuous." This issue comes up strongly when we discuss judgment. Although it may be difficult to "teach" someone how to make good decisions, there are rational steps we can take to ensure success. Also, we must realize that judgment is enhanced through experience in rendering decisions, especially in learning from our mistakes.

Here are a few suggestions for enhancing better judgment:

• Weigh the facts, reflect, and then act. Learn from the experience. If you've made a mistake, identify what you should have done differently and what you can do next time.

• Role-play scenarios that require decision making.

• Observe leaders you respect, and watch and reflect upon the decisions they make. What can you learn from them?

## Enthusiasm

Enthusiasm doesn't mean you have to shout or raise your voice. Enthusiasm refers to passion. How passionate are you about what you do? How do you demonstrate that passion? It's extremely important for you to find things you are passionate about because that passion becomes an intrinsic part of you and is readily noticed by other people. The suggestion here is quite simple. If you don't enjoy coming to work, if you don't enjoy coordinating events, if you don't like people, then it may be time to find another profession. If you are burned out or don't think that educational leadership is exciting and very rewarding, you cannot be an effective leader. Of course, we can't be equally passionate about everything. So identify those areas or projects you are most interested in and pursue them vigorously. Then, just watch your enthusiasm soar.

## Humility

Accept the things you cannot do. Most educators are self-confident practitioners, otherwise they wouldn't have entered the profession. We must, however, realize that we need assistance from others to do the important tasks that are required in education. How do we learn to appreciate our limitations?

• Listen to others and learn.

• Appreciate the importance of lifelong learning.

• Realize that you are replaceable. Those Dynamics, Aggressives, and Assertives need to accept one basic fact—after you're gone (either through retirement or death), the system will endure; life will go on. Contemplating that fact is a humbling experience. Meanwhile, make a difference by learning from and sharing with others.

### Imagination

If someone who is imaginative can see things that no one else can see, then how can those who can't see ever become imaginative? The truth of the matter is that you probably can't. Some people are naturally imaginative. However, there are things you can do to enhance your imaginative powers:

- Read books outside your field of specialization. I often read books on Buddhism or shipbuilding, areas in which I have little experience, simply to stir my imagination.
- Play games (any games, including cards, video games, or board games).
- Learn some magic tricks.
- Read a book on critical thinking.
- Interview someone you consider to possess great imagination. What can you learn from her?

## Tips for Identifying Virtues in Others

Although all virtues are important, one or more virtues may be particularly relevant for a specific position. For instance, if a school or district needs a principal or superintendent primarily to infuse the system with new ideas, then identifying a candidate who possesses imagination is most important. Knowing why a virtue is important for a particular situation is the first step toward seeking that virtue in others.

### Learn the Characteristics of Each Virtue

What do courageous people look like? How can you find out what virtues a candidate possesses? The best advice is to listen to the candidate, ask him questions that would compel him to relate scenarios and experiences, hear how he responds (e.g., does he credit only himself?).

You can also apply the definitions of the virtues to guide you in identifying the virtues exhibited by other people:

- Courage. Do they stand behind their principles?
- Impartial. Are they committed to maintaining a nonpartisan position in regard to controversial issues or problems?
- Empathy. Can they sense, identify with, and understand what another person is feeling?
- Judgment. Are the decisions they make decisive and accurate?
- Enthusiasm. Do they exude fervor about what they do?
- Humility. Are they aware of their limitations and at the same time cognizant of their strengths?
- Imagination. Do they have the ability to see what others can't?

Beyond the applying the definition of each virtue, you may find it helpful to use the following techniques to identify virtues.

- Ask others. Collect additional evidence about the individual. Ask former employers or other references specific questions such as, "Can you tell me about a time when Mr. Jones remained impartial in a situation that required the ability to sift through many conflicting pieces of evidence?"
- Ask the candidates. Simply ask the candidates to describe previous behaviors that demonstrated a particular virtue. Listen for detailed and descriptive statements. Ask yourself, "Do they seem sincere? Does the scenario appear real?" Don't be afraid to use your best judgment. The problem is that many of us are afraid to pose questions that may uncover virtues that are essential to good leadership. If we don't inquire at the hiring stage, then we shouldn't be surprised when a candidate does not demonstrate a particular virtue. Remember, an essential premise is that we too often focus on knowledge and skill competencies and not nearly enough on these virtues.
- See if actions speak louder than words. Asking candidates if they are courageous or impartial does not tell you whether they possess that virtue. The essential question is posed to find out if they *act* courageously, impartially, or humbly. Learn to become an observer of people's actions. Step back, watch, and learn.

The virtues of a leader are those that enable her to achieve excellence in that role. These virtues are desirable in themselves, revealing aspects of the leader as an educated individual and an admirable person. They are also effective in creating the conditions and context that can promote the goal of the organization and of education in general.

# 19

## Applying Leadership Potential

Warren Bennis (1989) said that the point "is not to become a leader. The point is to become yourself, to use yourself completely—all your skills, gifts, and qualities—in order to make your vision manifest. You must withhold nothing. You must, in sum, become the person you started out to be, and enjoy the process of becoming" (pp. 111–112). This statement is a good summary of the thrust of this book. Good leaders know themselves and use their talents (qualities and virtues) to improve schools (e.g., Buckingham & Clifton, 2001). Although you are who you are, as Bennis says, you can "become"—you can grow and improve and become an even better leader.

Moxley (2000) explained that self-knowledge is an "important attribute of those who engage in the activities of leadership. Our identity helps determine how we understand and practice leadership and engage in relationships that are integral to it. Individuals engaged in the practice of leadership must know their strengths and weaknesses, their personality preferences, what drives and motivates them, and how they have an impact on others" (p. 112). These are the messages I have tried to amplify in this book.

Self-awareness—the ability to form and understand identity—is critical to good leadership. The qualities and virtues we possess shape us. They identify who we are and what we can do. Understanding our qualities and virtues is the core to understanding ourselves. Daresh (1996) posited that "knowing oneself" was essential, perhaps even more so than knowing "how to do the job." Aristotle made the point even stronger, "The unexamined life is not worth living."

## Identifying the Leadership Team

Leadership entails people of different qualities working together toward a shared goal. Leadership does not focus solely on the capacity of one person, usually called the "boss." (A "boss" is usually a Dynamic Aggressive, although the leadership quality depends on the context.) Although a boss is the staple of most organizations, other individuals with different characteristics or qualities are equally essential. Leadership in this sense is a broad, inclusive activity in which combinations of quality groups work together toward a common goal.

Working together toward this goal presupposes that we have identified all the right individuals for a particular task or situation. Good leaders ask, "Do we need an architect (Dynamic Aggressive)? An innovator (Dynamic Assertive)? A stabilizer (Adaptive Assertive)? A campaigner (Adaptive Aggressive)? A healer (Dynamic Supportive)? A designer (Creative Assertive)? A sustainer (Adaptive Supportive)?" How we match the leadership quality (style, character, personality) of an individual to the needs of the situation is critical for effective leadership.

### From Theory to Practice

Sandra Braithwaite is superintendent of a large inner city school district that has nearly 11,000 students in grades K–12. She is a take-charge, visionary leader (a Dynamic Assertive) who has recently been appointed to revitalize the district. Specifically charged by the chancellor to improve reading and math scores and raise achievement levels across the curriculum, Braithwaite decides to put together a leadership team to spearhead reform efforts. Her goal is to build a learning community by developing and nurturing connections among people, socially and intellectually. At a staff meeting, she explains, "Building a learning community is tantamount to developing a commitment to shared learning." Identifying that the way to raise student achievement is to focus on instructional leadership, Braithwaite knows to appoint principals and assistant principals with a strong commitment to instructional improvement. Past practices in the district, however, relied on hiring supervisors who were good managers and not necessarily effective instructional leaders. Given that history, Braithwaite realizes that emerging trends in supervisory practice must emphasize (1) training for administrators as well as teachers in supervision, mentoring, and coaching; (2) sensitivity to the processes of professional growth and continual improvement; (3) training in observation and reflection on practice; (4) integration of supervision with staff development, curriculum development, and school improvement systems; and (4) collegial assistance among educators, parents, and students. In sum, she wants leaders who believe that supervision of instruction must be collaborative, collegial, and democratic.

While Braithwaite is familiar with the literature on instructional improvement, she is equally conversant in the theories of natural leadership qualities and virtues and is now ready to put the ideas into action. She knows that many educators have the requisite knowledge and skills to enhance instructional leadership, but she wonders if they are in the right positions to transform knowledge into action. Braithwaite understands that espousing a democratic and collaborative vision is very different from making it a reality and recognizes the political dimension involved in transforming a school or a district. Leaders who understand this political dimension and have the courage and imagination to make tough decisions are required.

Braithwaite has been given authority to appoint a cadre of leaders for the district office and to hire interim principals. She has a list of two dozen candidates with proven records of performance as strong instructional leaders to begin a situational evaluation. Braithwaite knows that an effective principal in an affluent neighborhood with multiple resources and a majority of untenured teachers may be less effective in an inner city neighborhood with fewer resources and a majority of tenured teachers. Armed with N.L.Q. and leadership virtues theories, Braithwaite begins to match individual strengths with situational requirements. Although certainly not an exact science, such an undertaking is guided by several key questions.

• What are the position vacancies (principal vacancies and positions in the district office)?

• What are the unique needs of each school (considering demographics, teachers' experience levels, achievement scores, current instructional programs, and PTA membership)? What kind of team does she need in the district office to carry out new instructional policies?

• What are the specific challenges in each school (e.g., is the school in disarray organizationally, does the school lack visionary leadership, are teachers complacent and lack motivation)? What is the heart of the problem in each school?

• What are the unique strengths of each candidate (principal and district leader)?

Braithwaite identifies characteristics she deems necessary for each school. In fact, she makes a grid that identifies each school and lists three major areas that would make it more effective. For example, School X has a sound curriculum, sufficient instructional materials, and adequate person-power, but lacks a leader who can empower other leaders to form a learning community. She then lists each principal candidate, along with that person's strongest quality. School X, according to Braithwaite, needs a Dynamic Assertive leader who can rock the boat and motivate others to a collective vision. The candidate must demonstrate, above all else, the courage to make tough and appropriate decisions that may well upset taken-for-granted practices and programs.

Meanwhile, Candidate A is an Adaptive Assertive. Despite many years of excellent service and outstanding organizational skills, he is the wrong leader for School X. He would be better suited in School Y, which needs someone who can coordinate and organize instructional activities in a coherent fashion. And in School Z, a Dynamic Supportive leader who displays impartiality and empathy is a better match because the school needs someone who can help reestablish interpersonal relationships among the faculty.

As far as her team in the district office is concerned, Braithwaite establishes goals and objectives for each position and then matches the qualities to the position. For example, she wants a few team members who are expert instructional leaders and who can relate to teachers in a supportive manner. Thus she may decide to select a Dynamic Supportive or an Adaptive Supportive individual to fill these positions. Braithwaite needs an individual to wade through the politics and opposition that inevitably arise in every change effort. Therefore, she needs to find an Adaptive Aggressive to ensure that the vision becomes a reality.

Braithwaite knows that she wants leaders, not followers. She wants to empower her leadership team so that they can empower others. Developing a learning community where the individual strengths of all educators are identified, valued, and nurtured is central to her task. Effective leadership relies on individuals of different qualities working together toward a shared goal.

Ralph Ryland works for an innovative school district that actively recruits its own employees for higher-level leadership positions. As assistant director of human resources in charge of recruitment at Great Lakes School District, Ryland's major responsibility is to identify individuals in the district who demonstrate leadership potential. Ryland recognizes that educational leaders must develop competencies in three interrelated dimensions: educational leadership, managerial competency, and political/leadership ability. Each dimension involves philosophical, social, and psychological perspectives, as well as technical competencies. See Figure 19.1 for a description of the dimensions critical for all leaders.

Ryland believes that candidates for leadership positions can learn these competencies in schools of education at a local university and through a meaningful internship practice in a school or district office. He also believes, however, that natural dispositions and characteristics determine who ultimately becomes an effective leader. "You can train almost anyone in the logistics of running a school or district such as learning how to develop a budget or complete attendance reports," explains Ryland. He continues, "What I look for in a candidate is what others are afraid to look for. I look for her natural inclinations and character traits. You can't train someone to be imaginative, compassionate, or dynamic. Educational leaders must possess unique characteristics."

He also explains that the characteristics he identifies are closely matched to the values espoused by the district.

In the recruitment process, Ryland always looks for several characteristics. First, individuals need to have strong sense of who they really are and what they can offer in terms of leadership. Beyond this, Ryland explains, "They need interpersonal skills, they need to be confident, and they need to think critically. Next, because the district is diverse and values its multicultural curriculum, individuals need to be open to varied perspectives and to be willing to confront prejudice and discrimination in the workplace." Ryland explains that in an interview he looks for these particular characteristics in the people he recommends. He concludes, "These characteristics are more important to me than the number of graduate credits a candidate completes in a graduate program."

## More on Team Leadership

Most situations do not call for the leadership of an isolated individual. Fundamentally, leadership is a partnership. It is critical to select the right combination of quality types to complete a particular task. Under traditional leadership practices, one leader is hired or charged to

---

**Figure 19.1**
**Competencies for Educational Leaders**

| Foundations & Philosophy | Managerial Competency | Political & Leadership Ability |
|---|---|---|
| Learning | Information manage- | Strategic planning |
| Teaching and | ment and use | Problem analysis and |
| instruction | Law and policy | decision making |
| Curriculum | Plant and facilities | Conflict resolution |
| Research | Finance | Change management |
| Teacher supervision | Personnel | Community relations |
| Instructional evaluation | Labor relations | Organizational theory |
| Staff development and | Technology as an | |
| Program evaluation | administrative tool | |

---

complete or direct the task and he tries to rally others to support his view. Leadership, however, is better conceived and conducted by a team, comprised of individuals possessing unique and distinct talents. We may, of course, need a Dynamic Aggressive to articulate the vision for what must be done, whose charisma attracts others to join the venture. A Creative Assertive can conceive the strategy for dealing with the task, but may stop short of knowing how best to implement the project. Organizing a successful program may fall to an Adaptive Assertive. An Adaptive Supportive can monitor the progress of students through the program, while a Dynamic Supportive offers guidance and assistance to individual students.

Team leadership does not necessarily replace the traditional hierarchy practiced in schools. Using team leadership within a traditional school structure, the person chiefly designated with authority (e.g., a principal or superintendent) can use knowledge about efficacy of leadership qualities and virtues to identify individuals best able to address specific needs. Although one leader in the educational hierarchy is primarily responsible and accountable, effective leadership is a shared activity that taps into the talents, qualities, and virtues of the many. Roland Barth (2001) agrees, "School leadership that must be managed by the principal constitutes only a fraction of the leadership available" (p. 444).

## Team Leadership in Action

The International High School (IHS), a multicultural alternative educational environment for recent arrivals to the United States, serves students with varying degrees of limited English proficiency. A collaborative project between the New York City Board of Education and LaGuardia Community College of the City University of New York, this school offers a high school and college curriculum combining substantive study of all subject matter with intensive study and reinforcement of English. The school's mission is to enable each student to develop the linguistic, cognitive, and cultural skills necessary for success in high school, college, and beyond.

IHS is a learning organization in which professional development is not a separate initiative but, rather, an integral part of the organization. The faculty and the student body are organized into six interdisciplinary teams. On each team, four teachers (math, science, English, and social studies teachers) and a support services coordinator are jointly responsible for a heterogeneous group of 75 school kids from 9th to 12th grade. The faculty works with the same group of students for a full year, providing a complete academic program organized around themes such as Motion, Conflict Resolution, or The American Dream. Teams also provide affective and academic counseling.

The interdisciplinary teams provide an ideal infrastructure for professional development. Significant decision-making power over curriculum, budget, and scheduling is delegated to the teams, and three hours of meeting time are built into each faculty team's weekly schedule. Team members use this time to develop and revise the curriculum, to plan schedules and allocate available resources, to discuss students with special needs and jointly devise ways of better meeting those needs, and to share successful practices and troubleshoot problems.

Team members also team-teach, particularly when new teachers are hired. The faculty evaluation process includes both self-evaluation and evaluation by peers on the team. The policy-setting body for the school is the Coordinating Council, which includes administrators, student government representatives, parents' association representatives, the union chapter leader, and a representative from each interdisciplinary team. Issues for the council may first surface in individual team discussions—for example, reporting on a successful innovation by one team for possible adoption schoolwide. Conversely, the council regularly identifies schoolwide issues that need discussion and action at the team level, such as how best to provide guidance services or how to align the curriculum offered by each team with state and city graduation standards. The council meets at least monthly. A steering committee, comprising the school's principal and two assistant principals and two elected teacher representatives, takes care of day-to-day school management and sets agendas for Coordinating Council meetings.

A team approach to professional development succeeds because it

• Starts with the belief that leadership is a team responsibility and that leadership may emerge from any quarter of the school.

• Is built, seamlessly, into the governance and instructional organization of the school.

• Gives teachers the necessary time and decision-making authority to support each other's professional development on and across teams.

• Supports individual professional growth and the sharing of best practice through peer coaching and evaluation by other team members, regularly scheduled teacher portfolio presentations, and team-teaching opportunities for new faculty members.

• Provides regular opportunities for collegial collaboration and the sharing of successful practice both within the school and with other schools serving similar students.

• Allows for regular, systematic interaction with the college and with businesses and community organizations, helping faculty constantly reassess how to prepare students for higher education and the world of work.

• Shares best practices with the larger educational community by hosting a constant flow of visitors, collaborating with outside researchers, being a member of citywide and national networks, and having faculty participate as instructors in various university teacher education programs and presenters at a wide range of conferences.

• Contains content that was determined collaboratively by representative bodies based on the school community's ongoing assessment of the instructional program.

• Promotes a climate of inquiry and continual improvement, as evidenced by a series of performance-driven organizational reforms implemented over the past 14 years.

• Is driven by a coherent long-term strategy, which uses graduation requirements to ensure that all students are able to meet rigorous graduation criteria.

The role of the principal in a faculty-governed school is interesting. Eric Nadelstern, the current and founding principal of IHS, is fond of saying the most important role he plays in the 14th year of the school is that of keeping someone else from sitting in his office (Nadelstern, Price, & Listhaus, 2000). In more reflective moments, he points out that the principal's role in a consensually governed school community is to provide teachers with the support necessary to be as good as they are, and to continuously remind them just how good that is. The principal

- Establishes a schoolwide expectation that leadership is a shared responsibility
- Acknowledges and establishes that he holds only a fraction of the leadership necessary for effective schooling
- Empowers everyone to assume responsibility for some form of leadership
- Focuses the school community on teaching and learning
- Builds a powerful community of leaders and learners
- Models in interactions with teachers the kind of relationships they should develop with students
- Develops a collegial vision and purpose
- Serves as a resource for solving problems and implementing new programs
- Assists faculty with their growth and development
- Evaluates new initiatives in relation to student learning outcomes
- Communicates the mission and philosophy of the school to internal and external audiences
- Enlists a broad base of political and financial support for ongoing experimentation and innovation

Democratic schools require stronger leadership than traditional, top-down, autocratic institutions. The nature of that leadership, however, is markedly different, replacing the need to control with the desire to support. Ironically, such leaders exercise much more influence where it counts, creating dynamic relationships between teachers and students in the classroom, and resulting in high standards of academic achievement.

There is no magic wand that creates a good leader. We need to appreciate and understand that leadership potential exists in all educators. The question is how best to develop the knowledge, skills, and, especially, dispositions needed to fill the leadership vacuum that exists in our schools.

# APPENDIX A:
## Assessing Your Natural Leadership Qualities

This survey contains 56 statements. Consider each statement and write a T (True) on the blank next to it if the statement describes you or the way you think you are. Write an F (false) next to each statement that does not describe you. Some statements may be difficult to classify, but please provide just one answer.

Your responses are anonymous. The surveys cannot accurately assess these attributes without your forthright responses to the various statements. You need not share your responses with anyone. Obviously, the accuracy of these instruments is dependent both on the truthfulness of your responses and the degree to which you are aware that you possess or lack a certain attribute.

_____ 1. I feel I'm good at supervising a small group of people, and I enjoy doing so.

_____ 2. When I'm in a new situation, such as a new job setting or relationship, I spend a lot of time comparing it to situations I've been in previously.

_____ 3. I believe that respect for authority is one of the cornerstones of good character.

_____ 4. I enjoy thinking about large issues, such as how society is organized politically.

_____ 5. I get asked for help a lot, and have a hard time saying no.

_____ 6. Ever since childhood, I've always seemed to want more out of life than my peers did.

_____ 7. When I first enter a new environment, such as a workplace or a school, I make it a point to become acquainted with as many people as possible.

_____ 8. I rarely seek quiet.

_____ 9. I can work harder than most people, and I enjoy doing so.

_____ 10. When I meet people, I'll give them the benefit of the doubt; in other words, I'll like them until they give me a reason not to.

_____ 11. The idea of a lifelong and exclusive intimate partner doesn't seem desirable or realistic for me.

_____ 12. A lifelong relationship with a romantic partner is one of my goals.

_____ 13. I can sometimes work creatively at full throttle for hours on end and not notice the passage of time.

_____ 14. I believe that divorce is to be strongly avoided whenever possible.

_____ 15. I'll periodically go through extremely low-energy periods during which I have to remind myself that it's only a phase.

_____ 16. When it comes to spending and saving habits, I take pride in being more thrifty and less foolish than most people.

_____ 17. Being alone does not scare me; in fact I do some of my best thinking when I'm alone.

_____ 18. My extended family is the most important part of my social life.

_____ 19. I spend much less time than others do on what I consider pointless leisure pursuits, such as TV and movie watching; novel reading; and card, computer, or board game playing.

_____ 20. I procrastinate a lot.

_____ 21. My vacations are always highly structured; several days of just sitting in one place and vegetating would drive me crazy.

_____ 22. Directing a big job and supervising a lot of subordinates is my idea of a headache.

_____ 23. People usually like me.

_____ 24. I find myself getting frustrated because most people's world view is so limited.

_____ 25. Networking as a career and life tool is something that comes naturally to me.

_____ 26. I'm happiest interacting with people and aiding them in some way.

_____ 27. I have a drive to express my ideas and influence the thinking of others.

_____ 28. I find myself getting frustrated because most people operate at a slower pace than I do.

_____ 29. I find myself getting frustrated because most people are not on my mental wavelength.

_____ 30. I generally believe that if individuals behave outside the norms of society, they should be prepared to pay the price.

_____ 31. My home is more organized and cleaner than most homes in my neighborhood.

_____ 32. Holding one job for decades would be okay with me if the conditions were good and the boss was nice.

_____ 33. When tackling a problem or task, I'm usually less defeatist than others.

_____ 34. It sometimes takes an outside force to get me motivated because I tend to be satisfied with what I have.

_____ 35. I enjoy the feeling of my life going along at an even pace like a well-oiled machine; too many stops and starts and ups and downs would really upset me.

_____ 36. Trying to lengthen your life by eating the "right" foods doesn't make much sense to me because, when your time's up, your time's up.

_____ 37. I have no trouble getting people to listen to me and grasp what I'm saying.

_____ 38. I understand that detail work is what ultimately gets a job done, and I have the gumption and know-how to tackle details.

_____ 39. Working by myself is no problem; in fact, I prefer it.

____ 40. At times, ideas just "come to me," and if I can't put them down then and there on paper, canvas, or other medium, I'm uncomfortable.

____ 41. I could never be really happy working for someone else.

____ 42. I like associating with influential people and am not intimidated by them.

____ 43. I'm happiest moving and doing, as opposed to sitting and thinking.

____ 44. Throughout my life, people have called me one or more of the following: temperamental, moody, sad, flighty, different. I never really felt like I was "one of the boys (or girls)."

____ 45. People tell me I have a great sense of humor.

____ 46. I believe that blood is thicker than water and that it's more important to be loyal to your relatives than to your friends.

____ 47. I don't have much time or patience for long family gatherings, such as a whole afternoon spent celebrating Thanksgiving.

____ 48. The makeup of my social circle is constantly changing.

____ 49. Managing a big job and having subordinates carry out the detail work is my ideal kind of endeavor.

____ 50. I prefer to work at a job a set number of hours each day and then have the rest of the 24 hours for relaxation.

____ 51. I'm good at smoothing over others' conflicts and helping to mediate them.

____ 52. I thrive on setting goals for myself and then figuring out how to reach them; I can't imagine just drifting through life without a plan.

____ 53. I'm more intelligent than most people, and others almost always recognize this.

____ 54. I can't fathom the idea of holding one job for decades.

____ 55. I find competition distasteful.

____ 56. I would never dress in a flashy, bohemian, or otherwise attention-getting way.

## Compiling Your Responses

The numbers in the table on the Answer Sheet correspond to the numbers of the survey statements. Marking on the table, circle the number of those statements that you recorded as True.

| **Answer Sheet** | | | | | | | | |
|---|---|---|---|---|---|---|---|---|
| Adaptive Assertive | 1 | 14 | 16 | 30 | 31 | 35 | 38 | 56 |
| Creative Assertive | 2 | 13 | 15 | 29 | 39 | 40 | 44 | 55 |
| Adaptive Supportive | 3 | 12 | 18 | 22 | 32 | 36 | 46 | 50 |
| Dynamic Assertive | 4 | 11 | 17 | 24 | 27 | 37 | 48 | 54 |
| Dynamic Supportive | 5 | 10 | 20 | 23 | 26 | 34 | 45 | 51 |
| Dynamic Aggressive | 6 | 9 | 19 | 28 | 41 | 47 | 49 | 53 |
| Adaptive Aggressive | 7 | 8 | 21 | 25 | 33 | 42 | 43 | 52 |

To tabulate the results, count the number of circled (true) responses in each category (e.g., the Adaptive Assertive row). Record that number on the table called Determining Your Quality Type as a fraction of 8. Thus the numerator of the fraction represents the number of circled or true responses, and the denominator represents the total number of questions on the survey related to that quality. For example, if you recorded true responses for seven out of the eight items in the first row, Adaptive Assertive, then your fraction would be 7/8.

Your Natural Leadership Quality is found under the category in which you scored the highest number of true responses. For example, if you scored 8/8 for Dynamic Supportive, then that is your quality. Perhaps no category earned an 8/8, but one category (e.g., Creative Assertive) had 7/8, whereas all the others were lower (6/8 and less). In that case, your quality is Creative Assertive.

| Determining Your Quality Type | |
|---|---|
| | ?/8 |
| Adaptive Assertive | |
| Creative Assertive | |
| Adaptive Supportive | |
| Dynamic Assertive | |
| Dynamic Supportive | |
| Dynamic Aggressive | |
| Adaptive Aggressive | — |

? = the number of true, circled responses in each row.

Although most respondents find their highest score in one category, some respondents may have two or more categories with the highest scores. For example, you may have scored 8/8 in two categories. If so, then your quality is represented by those two categories. If no category received an 8/8, locate the next highest score. If, for example, your highest score was a 5/8 and three categories may have earned that score, then your quality is represented by those three categories.

The meaning of these results will become clear as you read the book, beginning with the Introduction. *Please note:* No one assessment can accurately evaluate a person's inclinations or abilities. These surveys are meant to stimulate interest, thought, and discussion for purposes of exploring leadership in schools. Examine the results in light of the theories and ideas expressed in the book and make your own determination of their relevance and applicability to you personally and to your work in schools.

**Next, proceed to Appendix B and complete the surveys there.**

Source: Adapted with permission by Gary Null, from *Who Are You, Really? Understanding Your Life's Energy* (1996).

# APPENDIX B:
## Assessing Your Natural Leadership Virtues

There are four types of surveys in this Appendix. Complete all of them before reading the Preface and the Introduction to avoid skewing your results.

### Survey 1. What Are the Virtues of a Good Leader?

Brainstorm your best answers to the question, What are the virtues of a good leader? Note that the word *virtues* may be defined variously by different people. What does the word mean to you? In most instances, several one-word answers or descriptions suffice.

_____

_____

_____

While considering your answers, keep in mind that the word *good* is meant in the moral, ethical, and spiritual sense. So, for example, a dictator or autocratic leader would not represent a *good* leader. In addition, the word *leader* should be thought of in the generic sense, as opposed to a particular type of leader.

Now, answer the question by prioritizing your list (e.g., your first answer is the most important virtue of a good leader, your second answer is the next most important virtue). List no more than seven virtues.

_____

_____

_____

_____

_____

_____

_____

_____

## Survey 2. Virtues in Action

For each virtue you identified, please provide one brief description of a person you know who exemplifies that particular virtue. If necessary, select a famous leader or someone you know about, but do not know personally. For example, if you noted that "fairness" was one of the virtues, then mention a person (e.g., a superintendent you know) and describe how she demonstrates fairness. Be specific and brief. You may want to highlight an instance or situation that illustrates the virtue.

_____

_____

_____

_____

_____

_____

_____

## Survey 3. Assessing Your Leadership Virtues

This survey also contains 56 statements. Consider each statement and write a T (true) next to it if you think it describes you or the way you think you are. Write an F (false) next to each statement that does not describe you. Some statements may be difficult to classify, but please provide just one answer.

Your responses are anonymous. The surveys cannot accurately assess these attributes without your forthright responses to the various statements. You need not share your responses with anyone. Obviously, the accuracy of these instruments is dependent both on the truthfulness of your responses and the degree to which you are aware that you possess or lack a certain attribute.

_____ 1. If an injustice occurred, I would take action to remedy the situation even though such action might negatively affect my reputation in the educational community.

_____ 2. I acknowledge another point of view when data indicate that the other position is more accurate.

_____ 3. When I hear about another's suffering I am emotionally moved.

_____ 4. I do not have a problem rendering a decision once I have weighed all the facts.

_____ 5. I possess above-average levels of competence in almost any endeavor I undertake.

_____ 6. I do not flaunt my accomplishments. I do not like to be acknowledged for what I have done. I do not consider myself more competent than other educational leaders.

_____ 7. I easily formulate alternative solutions, think of questions, and design new ways of doing things.

_____ 8. If I knew that a child had been tracked in a lower ability group due solely to her ethnicity, I would speak out and attract attention to this injustice.

_____ 9. When I make up my mind about an important educational issue or matter, I easily alter my stance if information is presented contrary to my stance.

_____ 10. I demonstrate my compassion toward others (who are not part of my immediate family) by truly offering assistance and going out of my way to do so.

_____ 11. One of my major strengths, confirmed by people I know, is that I am a good judge of character.

_____ 12. I am a highly motivated, devoted, and ardent individual.

_____ 13. I do not deserve recognition or deference from others because of my training, knowledge, and experience.

_____ 14. I get bored quickly while performing detailed tasks and responsibilities.

_____ 15. I would speak out against any injustice even though I might face possible dismissal or public revilement.

_____ 16. In making decisions, I can absorb varied positions and pieces of evidence and remain neutral until rendering a final decision, even in cases in which I may have vested interests.

_____ 17. I often think or meditate about the welfare of others and wish them the best of luck.

_____ 18. I value openness to participation, diversity, conflict, and reflection.

_____ 19. Strong values and a commitment to actualize them motivate me.

_____ 20. I alter my beliefs when evidence is presented to contradict them.

_____ 21. I easily think of numerous possibilities or alternatives to problems.

_____ 22. A school board member asks me to hire a member of his family as a new teacher, but I believe this relative is inferior to another candidate. Despite pressures from the board member, I would decide not to hire the relative regardless of the consequences.

_____ 23. Despite natural inclinations, I would not favor someone from my ethnic group in rendering a decision about an educational matter.

_____ 24. I would give a friend the shirt off my back.

_____ 25. I am committed to consensus building.

_____ 26. Although not a fanatic, I have a strong commitment to see things through to the end.

_____ 27. I experience feelings of doubt about my job performance.

_____ 28. I possess initiative, independence, and creativity.

_____ 29. The school board wants to remove Harper Lee's novel *To Kill a Mockingbird* because the book has received complaints of racism. I feel that the charge of racism is misguided and would therefore decide not to remove the book.

_____ 30. I am not stubbornly close-minded even if I believe I am right.

_____ 31. I value commitment to the development of the individual within the school or district and I value treating all individuals as significant stakeholders in the organization.

_____ 32. I work hard to develop evaluative criteria to measure attainment of stated objectives.

_____ 33. People often tell me that I am passionate in whatever I do as opposed to being laid back.

_____ 34. I usually welcome and accept criticism.

_____ 35. People often consult me because they think I possess great imagination and creativity.

_____ 36. At an important meeting to decide the selection of a new textbook series, my colleagues protest the new textbook. However, I strongly feel that the school or district should adopt the book. Despite counterarguments by the opposing side, which represents an overwhelming majority, I would remain adamant and resist efforts by the opposition.

_____ 37. I do not consciously make prejudgments about people.

_____ 38. I openly give recognition to people for outstanding professional performance because I sincerely want to acknowledge their contributions.

_____ 39. I have no problem delegating authority in areas of responsibility to capable subordinates and then holding them accountable for results.

_____ 40. I dislike laziness and procrastination.

_____ 41. I usually admit ignorance and say, "I don't know" when I really don't know something.

_____ 42. Whenever confronted with a problem, I nearly always think "outside the box" initially.

_____ 43. I discover that several of the best starters on the school's basketball team ransacked the girl's locker room (although no girls were present) and did minor damage. The team is scheduled for the playoffs. I could overlook this infraction, but instead I decide to bench the offenders and thereby likely lose the game despite the protests of the other players, parents, and coaches.

_____ 44. I am usually consulted because people consider me fair and nonjudgmental.

_____ 45. Others would characterize me as a person who is kind, caring, nurturing, and sensitive.

_____ 46. I don't jump to conclusions and really try to judge everyone favorably.

_____ 47. I tend to see the glass half-full instead of half-empty.

_____ 48. I have several limitations, but try to accentuate my strengths.

_____ 49. When I participate in committee work, I usually come up with innovative suggestions.

_____ 50. Fellow educational leaders request that I represent them in a contractual dispute. However, I feel that their requests are unreasonable and perhaps unethical. I would decide not to represent them in negotiations.

_____ 51. I value honesty in words and action, and I have an unwavering commitment to ethical conduct.

_____ 52. I am responsive and sensitive to the social and economic conditions of students, as well as to their racial, ethnic, and cultural backgrounds.

_____ 53. I am mentally and emotionally centered and can think clearly about the best course of action to take, even in the face of criticism, insults, nagging, or negativity.

_____ 54. Others would characterize me as resilient, alert, optimistic, and even, at times, humorous.

_____ 55. Without my leadership assistance, things could still get accomplished.

_____ 56. When people tell me that something is impossible or unlikely, I immediately proceed to think of successful options.

### Understanding the Responses to Survey 3

The numbers in the table on the Answer Sheet correspond to the numbers of the survey statements. Marking on the table, circle the numbers of those statements that you recorded as True.

To tabulate the results, count the number of circled responses in each row (e.g., courage). Record that number in the table called Determining Your Virtues as a fraction of 8. Thus the numerator of the fraction represents the number of true or circled responses and the denominator represents the total number of questions on the survey (each survey has eight questions). For example, if you recorded true responses for seven out of the eight items in the first row, courage, then your fraction is 7/8.

| *Answer Sheet for Survey 3 Assessing Your Leadership Virtues* | | | | | | | | |
|---|---|---|---|---|---|---|---|---|
| Courage | 1 | 8 | 15 | 22 | 29 | 36 | 43 | 50 |
| Impartiality | 2 | 9 | 16 | 23 | 30 | 37 | 44 | 51 |
| Empathy | 3 | 10 | 17 | 24 | 31 | 38 | 45 | 52 |
| Judgment | 4 | 11 | 18 | 25 | 32 | 39 | 46 | 53 |
| Enthusiasm | 5 | 12 | 19 | 26 | 33 | 40 | 47 | 54 |
| Humility | 6 | 13 | 20 | 27 | 34 | 41 | 48 | 55 |
| Imagination | 7 | 14 | 21 | 28 | 35 | 42 | 49 | 56 |

The extent to which you naturally possess certain areas of excellence or virtues is found under the category in which you scored a high percentage of true responses. For example, if you scored 8/8 for enthusiasm, then you are likely an "enthusiastic" individual. (See chapters 9–15 for information about virtues.) You may, however, score equally high in other areas. If you scored at least seven true responses for a particular category, you probably possess that particular virtue.

| Determining Your Virtues | |
|---|---|
| | ?/8 |
| Courage | |
| Impartiality | |
| Empathy | |
| Judgment | |
| Enthusiasm | |
| Humility | |
| Imagination | |

? = the number of true, circled responses in each column.

The meaning of these results will become clear as you read the book, beginning with the Introduction. *Please note:* No one assessment can accurately evaluate a person's inclinations or abilities. These surveys are meant to stimulate interest, thought, and discussion for purposes of exploring leadership in schools. Examine the results in light of the theories and ideas expressed in the book, and make your own determination of their relevance and applicability to you personally and to your work in schools.

## Survey 4. Comparing Virtues

*Finding Your Leadership Style: A Guide for Educators* identifies seven virtues of a good leader. Examine the list of virtues in the next paragraph and compare them to your list in Survey 1. Are any of your virtues subsumed under the list? Why do you think the virtues you identified were not included in the list of seven virtues? Do not alter your responses to the survey.

The seven virtues of a good leader, as identified in this book, are listed in order: courage, impartiality, empathy, judgment, enthusiasm, humility, and imagination.

**After completing these surveys, please proceed immediately to the Preface and the Introduction.**

# APPENDIX C:
## Feedback Form

Please fill out this brief feedback form to help me gather more data on the accuracy and relevance of the leadership qualities discussed in this book. Please respond, considering only your answers to the N.L.Q. Survey. If you shared the survey with other people, please ask them to complete a Feedback Form on their results.

Please indicate how you feel about each of the following statements by circling one of the following choices:

### SA = Strongly Agree; A = Agree;
### D = Disagree; SD = Strongly Disagree

1. The results of the N.L.Q. survey (see Appendix A) accurately assess my leadership style.

SA A D S

2. The N.L.Q. survey will come in handy in assessing my future leadership plans.

SA A D S

3. The N.L.Q. survey will come in handy in assessing the leadership styles of other people whom I advise or am in contact with.

SA A D S

Please complete the following questions.

The single N.L.Q. that received the most true responses was _____

_____

The two N.L.Q.'s that received the most true responses
(in other words, they were tied) were _____

_____

The three N.L.Q.'s that received the most true responses
(in other words, they were tied) were _____

_____

My current position (title) is _____

_____

I've held this position for _____ years.

My previous position (title) was _____

_____

I held that position for _____ years.

What position do you aspire to, if any?

_____

_____

Finally, assess the degree of success you are experiencing in your current position by circling one of the following choices.

A. Superior—Perfectly suited for this position

B. Satisfactory—Well-suited for this position

C. Satisfied—Although not well-suited for this position

D. Dissatisfied—Looking to change position

E. Other—Please state and explain.

_____

_____

_____

Please send me your responses on this Feedback Form. I will ensure that your responses remain confidential. Mail it to Jeffrey Glanz, Wagner College, One Campus Road, Staten Island, NY 10301 USA. Or fax the survey to the attention of Jeffrey Glanz at (718) 390-3456. If you would like to obtain a copy of the results of this survey, please include your mailing address and e-mail address. If you have questions about the Feedback Form, send an e-mail message to me at jglanz@wagner.edu.

# References

Allport, G. (1987). *The nature of prejudice*. Reading, MA: Addison-Wesley.

Armstrong, T. (1998). *Awakening genius in the classroom*. Alexandria, VA: Association for Supervision and Curriculum Development.

Banks, J. (1997). *Educating citizens in a multicultural society*. New York: Teachers College Press.

Barth, R. S. (2001). Teacher leader. *Phi Delta Kappan, 82*(6), 443–449.

Bass, B. M., & Stogdill, R. M. (1990). *Handbook of leadership*. New York: Free Press.

Beck, L. G. (1994). *Reclaiming educational administration as a caring profession*. New York: Teachers College Press.

Bennis, W. (1989). *On becoming a leader*. Reading, MA: Addison-Wesley.

Blasé, J., Blasé, J., Anderson, G. L., & Dungan, S. (1995). *Democratic principals in action: Eight pioneers*. Thousand Oaks, CA: Corwin.

Blasé, J., & Kirby, P. C. (2000). *Bringing out the best in teachers: What effective principals do*. Newbury Park, CA: Corwin.

Blumenthal, I. (2001, April). Imperatives of leadership. *Executive Excellence Newsletter, 18,* 19.

Brownstein, S. (1999). *Healing your back pain naturally: The mind-body program proven to work*. Gig Harbor, WA: Harbor Press.

Brunn, E., & Getzen, R. (1996). *The book of American values and virtues*. New York: Black Dog & Leventhal.

Buckingham, M., & Clifton, D. O. (2001). *Now, discover your strengths*. New York: Free Press.

Byrd, D. M., & McIntyre, D. J. (Eds.). (1997). *Research on the education of our nation's teachers: Teacher education yearbook* (Vol. V). Thousand Oaks, CA: Corwin.

Coles, R. (2000). *Lives of moral leadership*. New York: Random House.

Covey, S. R. (1990). *The 7 habits of highly effective people: Powerful lessons in personal change*. New York: Simon & Schuster.

Daresh, J. C. (1996, April). *Lessons for educational leadership from career preparation in law, medicine, and training for the priesthood*. Paper presented at the annual meeting of the American Educational Research Association, New York.

Drucker, P. F. (1999). *Management challenges for the 21st century*. New York: HarperBusiness.

Fullan, M. (1997). *What's worth fighting for in the principalship*. New York: Teachers College Press.

Gallos, J. (1991/1997). *An instructor's guide to effective teaching: Using Bolman and Deal's Reframing Organizations*. San Francisco: Jossey-Bass.

Gardner, H. (1995). *Leading minds: An anatomy of leadership*. New York: BasicBooks.

Gardner, J. W. (1990). *On leadership*. New York: Free Press.

Glanz, J. (1998). *Action research: An educational leader's guide to school improvement*. Norwood, MA: Christopher-Gordon.

Glanz, J. (1998). Multicultural education as a moral imperative: Affirming the diversity of ideas and perspectives. *Focus on Education, 42*, 18–24.

Glanz, J. (2002). Leading with soul and conviction: Effective leadership qualities and virtues [Speech]. At National Council of Professors of Educational Administration, Burlington, VT.

Glickman, C., & Mells, R. L. (1997). Why is advocacy for diversity a moral imperative. In J. Glanz, & R. F. Neville, *Educational Supervision* (pp. 341–348), Norwood, MA: Christopher-Gordon.

Goldberg, M. F. (2001). *Lessons from exceptional school leaders*. Alexandria, VA: Association for Supervision and Curriculum Development.

Goodlad, J. I., & McMannon, T. J. (Eds.). (1997). *The public purpose of education and schooling*. San Francisco: Jossey-Bass.

Haney, W. V. (1955). *Uncritical inference test*. Available from International Society for General Semantics, P.O. Box 728, Concord, CA 94522. Phone: 925-798-0311.

Hansen, J. H., Lifton, E. & Gant, J. (1999). *Leadership for continuous school improvement*. Swampscott, MA: Watersun.

Hare, W. (1993). *What makes a good teacher: Reflections on some characteristics central to the educational enterprise*. London: Althouse Press.

Jossey-Bass. (2000). *The Jossey-Bass reader on educational leadership*. San Francisco: Author.

Kaser, J., Mundry, S., Stiles, K., & Loucks-Horsley, S. (2001). *Leading every day: 124 actions for effective leadership*. Thousand Oaks, CA: Corwin.

Lambert, L. (1998). *Building leadership capacity in schools*. Alexandria, VA: Association for Supervision and Curriculum Development.

Lewin, R. (1993). *Complexity: Life at the edge of chaos*. London: Phoenix.

Lewis, B. A. (1998). *What do you stand for? A kid's guide to building character*. Minneapolis: Free Spirit.

Marshall, C. (1995). Imagining leadership. *Educational Administration Quarterly, 31*, 484–492.

Moxley, R. S. (2000). *Leadership and spirit: Breathing new vitality and quality into individuals and organizations*. San Francisco: Jossey-Bass.

Nadelstern, E., Price, J. R., & Listhaus, A. (2000). Student empowerment through the professional development of teachers. In J. Glanz. & L. S. Behar-Horenstein (Eds.), *Paradigm debates in curriculum and supervision* (pp. 265–275). Westport, CN: Bergin & Garvey.

Nieto, S. (1996). *Affirming diversity*. New York: Longman.

Noddings, N. (1984). *Caring: A feminist approach to ethics and moral education*. Berkeley: University of California Press.

Noddings, N. (1992). *The challenge to care in schools: An alternative approach to education*. New York: Teachers College Press.

Null, G. (1996). *Who are you, really? Understanding your life's energy*. New York: Carroll & Graf.

Osterman, K. F., & Kottkamp, R. B. (1993). *Reflective practice for educators: Improving schooling through professional development*. Newbury Park, CA: Corwin.

Paul, R. (1993). *Critical thinking: What every person needs to survive in a rapidly changing world*. Santa Rosa, CA: Foundation for Critical Thinking.

Palmer, P. J. (2002). *The courage to teach: Exploring the inner landscape of a teacher's life*. New York: Teachers College Press.

Patterson, J. L. (1993). *Leadership for tomorrow's schools*. Alexandria, VA: Association for Supervision and Curriculum Development.

Regan, H. B. (1990). Not for women only: School administration as a feminist activity. *Teachers College Record, 91*, 565–577.

Sadker, D. M., & Sadker, M. P. (1999). *Teachers, school, and society*. New York: McGraw-Hill.

Schon, D. A. (1987). *Educating the reflective practitioner: Toward a new design for thinking and learning in the professions*. San Francisco: Jossey-Bass.

Senge, P. (1990). *The fifth discipline*. New York: Doubleday.

Sergiovanni, T. J. (1992). *Moral leadership: Getting to the heart of school improvement*. San Francisco: Jossey-Bass.

Sergiovanni, T. J. (1996). *Leadership for the schoolhouse: How is it different? Why is it important?* San Francisco: Jossey-Bass.

Sergiovanni, T. J. (2000). *The lifeworld of leadership: Creating culture, community, and personal meaning in our schools*. San Francisco: Jossey-Bass.

Starratt, R. J. (1993). *The drama of leadership*. London: Falmer Press.

Starratt, R. J. (1996). *Transforming educational administration: Meaning, community, and excellence*. New York: McGraw-Hill.

Sullivan, S., & Glanz, J. (2000). *Supervision that improves teaching: Strategies and techniques*. Thousand Oaks, CA: Corwin.

# Index

# About the Author

Jeffrey Glanz is dean of graduate programs and head of the Department of Education at Wagner College in Staten Island, N.Y. Before arriving at Wagner, he served as executive assistant to the president of Kean University in Union, N.J., where he held faculty status as a tenured professor in the Department of Instruction and Educational Leadership, within the College of Education. Glanz was named Graduate Teacher of the Year in 1999 by the Student Graduate Association and was also that year's recipient of the Presidential Award for Outstanding Scholarship. Glanz served as an administrator and teacher in the New York City public schools for 20 years. He is the author of eight books and many peer-reviewed articles.

Glanz is an Adaptive Assertive and attributes his professional and personal successes to understanding and enhancing his natural leadership quality while maximizing his leadership virtues. You may contact him at jglanz@wagner.edu.

# Related ASCD Resources

Although only a few products are listed, ASCD offers numerous publications for teachers, teachers-in-training, and supervisors of teachers. At the time of publication, the following resources were available; for the most up-to-date information about ASCD resources, go to www.ascd.org. ASCD stock numbers are noted in parentheses.

## Networks

Visit the ASCD Web site (www.ascd.org) and use the search button to look for "networks," then go to About ASCD networks for information about professional educators who have formed groups around topics, such as "Affective Factors in Learning," "Mentoring Leadership and Resources," and "Performance Assessment for Leadership." Look in the Network Directory for current facilitators' addresses and phone numbers.

## Print Products

*A Better Beginning: Supporting and Mentoring New Teachers* by Marge Scherer (#199236)

*Classroom Instruction That Works: Research-Based Strategies for Increasing Student Achievement* by Robert J. Marzano, Debra J. Pickering, and Jane E. Pollock (#101010)

*Enhancing Professional Practice: A Framework for Teaching* by Charlotte Danielson (#196074)

*A Handbook for Classroom Instruction That Works* by Robert J. Marzano, Jennifer S. Norford, Diane E. Paynter, Debra J. Pickering, and Barbara B. Gaddy (#101041)

*How to Help Beginning Teachers Succeed,* 2nd ed., by Stephen P. Gordon and Susan Maxey (#100217)

*Qualities of Effective Teachers* by James H. Stronge (#102007)

*Teacher Evaluation/Teacher Portfolios* ASCD Electronic Topic Pack (#197202)

*A Teacher's Guide to Working with Paraeducators and Other Classroom Aides* by Jill Morgan and Betty Y. Ashbaker (#100236)

## Videotapes

The Teacher Series (series: two sets of 3 tapes each) (#401088, #401089)

For additional resources, visit us on the World Wide Web (http://www.ascd.org), send an e-mail message to member@ascd.org, call the ASCD Service Center (800-933-ASCD or 703-578-9600, then press 2), send a fax to 703-575-5400, or write to Information Services, ASCD, 1703 N. Beauregard St., Alexandria, VA 22311-1714 USA.